"The Psalms have always been my go·
ing desperate; the psalmists echo m
Howe captures vital snapshots to help us process these precious verses
in a way that helps hope take up residence in our lives to renew, restore,
redeem, and rejuvenate our heart, soul, mind, and life!'"

**Pam Farrel, best-selling author of over 50 books,
including *Discovering Hope in the Psalms***

"Prepare to be wowed! Michele Howe entices her readers into the Psalms
with her practical, reader-friendly style. I love how she always offers us
real-life examples and describes relatable struggles we all are familiar
with. She gently holds a mirror for us to see our weak responses to
difficult times: trusting our own hearts and emotions rather than truth,
becoming hopeless and forgetting God's loving grace and mercy, giving
in to anxiety, attacking others in anger, or refusing to forgive. She then
graciously draws us into the Psalms to seek and find answers that God
lovingly offers, righteously commands, practically teaches, and patiently
reminds us. You'll see the Psalms in a fresh and practical way. A must-read
for anyone struggling."

—Sarah Halsey, biblical counselor

"The Psalms seem to meet us right where we are at in life. They speak
to our emotions, comfort our hearts, and reassure us with hope. Most
importantly, the Psalms help us learn about the heart of God. I love the
way Michele walks us through specific psalms using stories and insights
to help us apply these truths to our daily lives. *Deliver Us* is a powerful
and positive book that will strengthen your passion for living with your
eyes looking to God in every area of your life."

—Karol Ladd, best-selling author of *The Power of a Positive Woman*

"Michele Howe's personal daily habit of reading the Psalms has brought
forth a wonderful collection of real-life stories that offer readers hope,
even as they face the most trying circumstances. As with her other books,
Michele relies on the best of remedies—the word of God—and serves
it up in a way that is fresh and—like its Author—makes all things new."

—Judy Roberts, journalist and former newspaper religion editor

"Howe reminds us that life can be messy. It is never pain free, conflict free, or without challenges. In *Deliver Us*, she writes, 'May each of us submit to whatever form of suffering and pain the Lord allows in our lives.' This is the crux of spiritual growth; not the absence of pain but our capacity and willingness to embrace it as a means to maturity. Her stories offer real-life examples of fellow travelers struggling with life's inevitable trials. But Howe doesn't leave us there. She gives us practical action, God's promises, and closing thoughts to ponder in each chapter."

—Don S. Otis, president of Veritas Communications and author of multiple books

"In every chapter, *Deliver Us* presents a true story of raw, personal struggle that finds expression in the Psalms, as misery is transformed into the experience of God's deliverance. With compelling quotes from famous Christians, prayers, and practical strategies for living the truths of Scripture, the author brings compassion to us with each true story. As you engage in this inspiring book, you will learn to think more biblically in your responses to life's trouble, which will bring God's loving and powerful deliverance to you."

—Maddie Walberg, biblical counselor

"Michele Howe is the go-to for hope and guidance in the seasons of life and heart. When crisis overwhelms, *Deliver Us* provides assurance that God sees you. Find peace in chaos, sense in the senseless, and rest in the promise that God is always with you and has already made a way."

—PeggySue Wells, best-selling author of 29 books, including *The Slave Across the Street*, *Chasing Sunrise*, and *Ten Best Decisions A Single Mom Can Make*

MICHELE HOWE

deliver us

Finding *Hope* in the Psalms
for Moments of Desperation

HENDRICKSON
PUBLISHERS

Deliver Us: Finding Hope in the Psalms for Moments of Desperation

© 2020 Michele Howe

Published by Hendrickson Publishers
an imprint of Hendrickson Publishing Group
Hendrickson Publishers, LLC
P. O. Box 3473
Peabody, Massachusetts 01961-3473
www.hendricksonpublishinggroup.com

ISBN 978-1-68307-307-9

Cover image: Sunset at the ocean in watercolor by evgenii141 via Adobe Stock

Printed in the United States of America

First Printing — July 2020

Library of Congress Control Number: 2020938263

I've long held the opinion that one of the most challenging (albeit eternally rewarding) responsibilities on earth is to serve in the role as a pastor's spouse. On that premise, I want to offer a heartfelt and resounding "Thank you!" to four women in my life who consistently go above and beyond the call of duty to serve the Lord, their husbands, their children (and grandchildren), their families and friends, and their local church body:

Amy English (my friend who serves at West Rockport Baptist Church)
Marcia Hinz (my friend who serves at Bedford Alliance Church)
Maddie Walberg (my friend who served at Berean Fellowship)
Nicole Zatko (my daughter who serves at Jericho Road Church)

I know that each of you has been a key component in helping to deliver those within your care from despair, depression, discouragement, and even death, as you passionately point everyone to Jesus, the Savior and Redeemer of our souls.

I dedicate this book to you. I love you all, and I'm so grateful to have been the happy recipient of your wisdom, compassion, and tender care.

⌒ Contents

Acknowledgments

As the classic Bob Dylan song goes, "The times, they are a-changin.'" So what better time than now to place the full weight of our hope and trust in the changeless character of our God (and his eternally unchanging promises). Who but God could have known that I personally would need to spend much more time deeply studying the book of Psalms at this particular season of my life? Some eighteen months ago, I started being drawn to this book in a deeper way. The reading of the Psalms then led to meditating on them, which in turn led me to wanting to write a book where a portion of a psalm would be the centerpiece of each story featured in this book. I am so grateful that Hendrickson Publishers agreed to take on this project with me.

As it is with every book I write, I am continually (and with increasing measure) amazed at the extraordinary talent the entire Hendrickson team extends to create the book that you, dear reader, now hold in your hands. If I may, I would like to name some names so you can be thankful right along with me for these tremendous individuals who give their best every day (on every book project) to create a resource worthy of the Hendrickson Publishers name. To start, I want to say a supersized "Thank you!" to editorial director (now friend) Patricia Anders, who does her marvelous editorial work on my books time and time again. I both respect and admire you (and your exemplary work ethic) to produce the finest books possible.

To Dave Pietrantonio, Hendrickson's book production manager, who organizes all the behind-the-scenes production details in a seemingly effortless way, my ongoing thanks and gratitude. To Meg Rusick, Phil Frank, and Tina Donohue: I love that you are the same wonderfully skilled group of people who labor hard each in your individual ways to bring together a book worth far more than its selling price. That's an amazing thing! I'm so thankful for each of you. Finally, my thanks and appreciation to my agent at the Steve Laube Agency, Bob Hostetler. You're always reminding me to dot my i's and cross my t's—and I thank you for that!

Lastly, no author can ever forget her readers. I'm humbled and grateful that the Lord has continued to allow me the privilege to write (and speak biblical truth) into people's lives about the wondrous power-working love of Jesus. Oh, what a Savior! May you find in him all that you long for and all that you need—for Jesus is our one and only Great Deliverer.

Whoever dwells in the shelter of the Most High
    will rest in the shadow of the Almighty
I will say of the LORD, "He is my refuge and my fortress,
    my God, in whom I trust."

Surely he will save you
    from the fowler's snare
    and from the deadly pestilence.
He will cover you with his feathers,
    and under his wings you will find refuge;
    his faithfulness will be your shield and rampart.
You will not fear the terror of night,
    nor the arrow that flies by day,
 nor the pestilence that stalks in the darkness,
    nor the plague that destroys at midday. . . .

"Because he loves me," says the LORD, "I will rescue him;
    I will protect him, for he acknowledges my name.
He will call on me, and I will answer him;
    I will be with him in trouble,
    I will deliver him and honor him.
With long life I will satisfy him
    and show him my salvation."

PSALM 91

Introduction

As this book is getting ready to go to the printer, we are all sheltering at home during what is called the COVID-19 (or coronavirus) pandemic. More than ever, we need the comfort we find from God through the Scriptures—particularly, the book of Psalms. It is amazing how perfectly Psalm 91 speaks to us in this current situation—and for other times when we suffer from "deadly pestilence" and "the plague that destroys at midday." As this psalm addresses diseases, such as this current virus that "stalks in the darkness," it also reminds us that God is our deliverer and our salvation, and in our moments of desperation, we know that he is our certain hope.

> Whoever dwells in the shelter of the Most High
> will rest in the shadow of the Almighty
> I will say of the Lord, "He is my refuge and my fortress,
> my God, in whom I trust."

For many years, I've made it my daily habit to read five corresponding psalms each day. Early on in my Christian walk, I was given a model for reading through the book of Psalms each month by reading the current day's psalm and then adding the number *30* to that particular day's date, five consecutive times. (Example: On June 1, read Psalms 1, 31, 61, 91, 121.) When following this pattern, you will read through all 150 psalms twelve times every year.

Once I adopted this helpful routine, I never looked back. This book of ancient yet astonishingly relevant poetry provides praise for when I'm feeling happy, content, joyful, or full of faith. But it also buoys me up emotionally when I'm feeling a lack of faith, angry, upset, irritated, scared, or ignored. I guess you can say that no matter what I'm feeling, there's a psalm for that!

I love it. It doesn't matter what circumstance I'm in, what challenges I'm facing, or what my next step is going to be, I can find the wisdom, understanding, knowledge, and loads of everyday encouragement by reading through the Psalms. I hope that as you take some time to read and meditate on the powerful, life-giving truths found throughout this book, you'll make the same discovery I did so many years ago. In the Psalms, we can find emotional deliverance from anything that life (or the enemy of our souls) throws at us.

As you read, you'll find real-life accounts of other believers who faced down their moments (or sometimes lingering seasons) of difficulties that bordered on seemingly impossible-to-conquer obstacles. But as they discovered (and as you will too), God has already provided us with everything we need for life and godliness through his word and the supernatural enabling of the Holy Spirit.

So, take some time to get away from whatever stresses and burdens you're carrying at this moment to reconnect with the living God. You will not be disappointed. And remember that no matter whatever trial you're in, whatever season of suffering you're enduring, whatever challenges you can't see past right now—there's a psalm for that!

As the deer pants for streams of water,
   so my soul pants for you, my God.
My soul thirsts for God, for the living God.
   When can I go and meet with God?
My tears have been my food
   day and night,
while people say to me all day long,
   "Where is your God?"
These things I remember
   as I pour out my soul:
how I used to go to the house of God
   under the protection of the Mighty One
with shouts of joy and praise
   among the festive throng. . . .

By day the LORD directs his love,
   at night his song is with me—
   a prayer to the God of my life.

Why, my soul, are you downcast?
   Why so disturbed within me?
Put your hope in God,
   for I will yet praise him,
   my Savior and my God.

PSALM 42

CHAPTER 1

Enduring the Valley of Depression

Perseverance asks the questions, "Today, how will I represent God? How will I trust him and follow him in obedience?" Then it asks for help from others, cries out to the Lord, and looks for an opportunity to love. It may seem feeble, but our confidence is in the God who is strong. The essence of persevering is trusting or obeying because of Jesus.

EDWARD T. WELCH

L eah woke up at her normal time, even though she hadn't worked for the past two months and could have slept late. Although she was only fifty-seven, she had taken the early retirement package offered at the factory where she had worked hard for over twenty-five years. She was pretty sure her employer would not offer such a generous benefits package again before her original retirement date in a few years, so she wanted to take advantage of it now.

But this was a huge step. To make sure she was acting wisely, she consulted her financial counselor and asked for advice from family and friends. All of them said she should go ahead and submit her retirement paperwork. That final week at work, Leah felt a few brief moments of panic, which made her worry about this life-altering decision. At this point, however, there was no going back, and she told herself that she'd be all right.

Ever since high school, Leah had lived within modest means—something she learned from her frugal parents, who taught her how to create a workable budget and stick to it. So money wasn't an issue. What Leah hadn't anticipated was how she would feel about not having that steady 7:30 a.m. to 3:30 p.m. job to go to every weekday year-round.

Eight long weeks after her last day of employment, Leah found herself depressed. She felt alone, adrift, unsure of what to do with herself in the coming months and years. After all, she was still relatively young and in good health. These past two months had been a welcome break from the old work routine that had become her life, but now she wanted to get on with something new. As a single woman, she had filled her weekdays with work, followed by busy weekends of house and yard chores. For the first time, she realized that she had never just sat down to think and be quiet—to really be alone with her own thoughts.

But then she rediscovered her old prayer journal. She dusted it off and read through some long-forgotten entries. Picking up her Bible, she turned instinctively to the Psalms, rereading her favorites, letting them speak to her in a way they never had before.

> These things I remember
> as I pour out my soul.

After some time reading and then praying and listening, she began to sense what God had for her next. She no longer felt alone or adrift.

> By day the LORD directs his love,
> at night his song is with me—
> a prayer to the God of my life.

Today, Leah's "new normal" entails getting up and taking a brisk walk around her neighborhood before coming back to spend quiet time with the Lord—and making it a daily habit to record in that old journal her prayers for her life for today and in the coming weeks and years. It is this precious time each morning that keeps Leah tethered to her only constant in life—God. She now realizes that for the first time in twenty-five years, she can focus on finally quenching that lifelong thirst.

> As the deer pants for streams of water,
> so my soul pants for you, my God.

7

As I considered Leah's unexpected season of depression, it didn't surprise me. All of us are creatures of habit. And even though we may not especially like or appreciate every component that makes up the whole of our daily lives, we get accustomed to the regularity of the parts and parcels that compose it. I've sat beside many an individual after a major life change (both the positive, planned ones and the difficult, unexpected ones) who find themselves unexpectedly mired in depression, especially those who feel lost like Leah. Most of these dear folks don't even understand why they're feeling as they do.

For my part, I remember enduring my own summer of depression after years of exhaustive caregiving, parenting our four teens, changing churches after a heartbreaking split, and then undergoing major surgery and subsequently not sleeping for weeks on end. It was as though my body finally gave voice to its exhaustion and screamed, "Enough!" I felt much as Leah did—adrift and untethered, either sobbing or just feeling numb. It was a dreadful and dark season in my life.

Thankfully, as Leah did, I returned to my one faithful and unchanging source: God. I recall sitting outside in the bright sunshine reading my Bible, memorizing God's promises, and praying for him to heal my sad and weary self. In time, he did heal me. But it was a long, arduous journey from which I learned life lessons I now treasure. I discovered anew God's faithfulness in a greater way than ever before. While my emotions were admittedly an unpredictable mess at times, I found God alone to be my strength, my redeemer, and my hour-by-hour grace giver.

I thank the good Lord that he surrounded me with godly friends who spoke truth into my fragile heart. As Leah discovered, when we feel lost or uncertain, we know we can count on our unchanging, always-faithful God to provide us with the grace we need to face each new day and whatever he has in store for us.

ᠼ Take-away Action Thought

When you feel the heavy weight of depression, tell yourself the truth you need to hear: Do not trust your volatile emotions during this season. Instead, turn to God's word every day and allow his magnificent promises to permeate your heart, mind, and soul. Spend time meditating on the unchanging, always-faithful character of your heavenly Father who promises to meet your every need.

My Heart's Cry to You, O Lord

Father, I never expected to feel depressed. I'm either crying tears apparently for no reason or I'm feeling nothing. I hate these extreme emotional swings. Please speak peace to my heart, mind, and soul. Help me to be self-disciplined to sit myself down and read the Bible every single day. Give me clarity of thought so I can meditate on your powerful promises. Please guide me as I pray and help me to listen. I ask for the healing of my heart and emotions. If there's something physically wrong with me, grant me wisdom on what to do about it. Whatever is going on, I know how much I need you to stay near me to comfort me in this dark season and guide me out of it. Amen.

Deliver Us

1. "As the deer pants for streams of water, so my soul pants for you, my God. My soul thirsts for God, for the living God." Despite how depressed you feel today, try to discipline yourself to spend time reading your Bible and praying. By faith, you can lean more intentionally into the love of God, no matter how extreme or powerful your emotions may be.

2. "By day the LORD directs his love, at night his song is with me—a prayer to the God of my life." Each day, spend a few moments

writing down specific ways you see the Lord demonstrating his love for you. Play worship music and concentrate on the lyrics that tell of God's unchanging, always-faithful character.

3. "Put your hope in God, for I will yet praise him, my Savior and my God." This week, find at least one person to serve in love. Prayerfully ask the Lord to provide you with an opportunity to give of your time and talents to another. By faith, you can trust the Lord to provide you with the strength you need to love and serve others well.

Listen to my prayer, O God,
    do not ignore my plea;
hear me and answer me.
My thoughts trouble me and I am distraught. . . .

I said, "Oh, that I had the wings of a dove!
    I would fly away and be at rest.
I would flee far away
    and stay in the desert;
I would hurry to my place of shelter,
    far from the tempest and storm." . . .

As for me, I call to God,
    and the LORD saves me.
Evening, morning and noon
    I cry out in distress,
    and he hears my voice. . . .

Cast your cares on the LORD
    and he will sustain you;
he will never let
    the righteous be shaken.

PSALM 55

CHAPTER 2

Loving a Special-Needs Child

When suffering shatters the carefully kept vase that is our lives, God stoops to pick up the pieces. But he doesn't put them back together as a restoration project patterned after our former selves. Instead, he sifts through the rubble and selects some of the shards as raw material for another project—a mosaic that tells the story of redemption.

KEN GIRE

Rachel sat down on a bench at the far edge of the playground and wept quietly. While this probably wasn't the time or place, it was good to release all that pent-up emotion. Pulling tissues from her backpack, she dabbed at her eyes and then tilted her head up toward the sky and cried out silently to the Lord again. *Please help me to have the strength I need to be the mom Asher deserves.*

She knew she had rushed into this adoption faster than might have been best, but she had to either take Asher home with her or possibly lose him to another adoptive family. What the adoption agency hadn't told her was the extent of the damage done to his little body while he was still in his mother's womb. No one told her that Asher was a heroin baby. But had she known this, would she have chosen any differently? She didn't think so. All she could do right now was pray for God's guidance on how to navigate the uncertain waters she was now treading with this child.

As Rachel's tears ceased, she felt drained but strangely relaxed, at peace. Looking around the playground, she noticed all the children running around and having fun—children no doubt from normal, healthy families. As they laughed and shouted to one another, Rachel could only imagine how Asher would react to all that noise and stimulus. Taking a deep breath, she replayed in her mind some recent scenes he had made. She had learned by now that whenever he became agitated by something, it quickly spiraled into aggression. Aware of how suddenly his moods could change, she was continually on guard, prepared to run interference between him and other children.

It wasn't long after she had adopted him that she began to notice that her new toddler son wasn't like the other children she knew. After she found out what was wrong with him, Rachel made the necessary adjustments and began to shelter Asher from anything that triggered these fear-driven responses. But as he grew older and his world expanded with school and sports, it had become more difficult for Rachel to protect the boy with special needs from life's many uncertainties.

Now at age seven, Asher was attending a small Christian school with a caring, dedicated teacher and staff, and the class sizes were ideal. Rachel was so hopeful that Asher would adjust to this new school scenario and thrive there. But then week after week, she began receiving calls from either his teacher or the school counselor. She had lost count of the number of times she sat in that counselor's office, trying to find new ways to help Asher overcome these behavioral and academic obstacles.

This afternoon, Rachel had received yet another summons to the office after Asher had scribbled all over his classmates' artwork displayed in their classroom. Of course, the other children were upset. Rightly so. But Rachel was at a loss how to reach into Asher's mind to get him to understand that his impulsive actions held consequences. At this point, she was afraid they were going to permanently suspend him and that she'd have to find yet another school.

Feeling better after that cry, she sighed as she looked up toward the sky and softly asked, "What now, Lord?" Although she knew better than to expect an audible answer, some kind of heavenly sign would be most welcome! As she continued sitting, she suddenly felt as if a still small voice told her to open her Bible. She pulled it out of the backpack and turned to her last bookmarked place, Psalm 55, and she began to read:

Listen to my prayer, O God,
  do not ignore my plea;
hear me and answer me.
My thoughts trouble me and I am distraught.

As she read, she felt again that peace flood through her, and somehow, she knew she would find a way to help Asher, to give him the love and support he needed. That they both needed.

As for me, I call to God,
  and the LORD saves me.
Evening, morning and noon
  I cry out in distress,
  and he hears my voice.

Rachel's story strikes a particular heartstring for me personally, because my brother and sister-in-law adopted two siblings, a boy and a girl, when they were twelve months and two and a half years old, respectively. Their mother was a heroin addict who had abandoned her young children to the care of their grandmother, who was a former heroin addict herself. When these little ones came into the lives of my brother and his family, my brother and his wife saw a need and met it. They were "all in" and fully committed to rescuing these children from the dire situation they had somehow managed to survive since birth. Like Rachel's son, Asher, my nephew has met with some learning challenges. But my sister-in-law, being a remarkable homeschooling director and now private school teacher, creatively forged a way for her son to learn and thrive.

Like Rachel, my sister-in-law can also tell you there were days (*many* days) when she wondered if she was up to the task of being a mother for these two young ones. My brother and sister-in-law already had two high schoolers of their own at the time of the adoption, so it was literally a family affair to make room for these needy children. I'll never forget one conversation I had with my sister-in-law after a particularly challenging parenting season. Her words to me were profound: "This is totally a God-thing. And I believe he is going to fully redeem every moment of suffering these two have suffered. Then watch out world!"

I know with certainty that Rachel and my brother and his family have repeatedly turned to the Lord for the grace, wisdom, and strength to love these special little ones. They courageously meet their special needs in special ways, even when they feel undone by exhaustion. I know this to be true, because they have told me so. These adoptive parents go directly to the source for their supernatural sustenance. Though the future may seem uncertain and even daunting, their confidence is in our unchanging and certain God.

Take-away Action Thought

When your circumstances overwhelm you, and you feel uncertain about what to do next, turn your heart and mind toward the Lord. Although you may cry out to him evening, morning, and noon, be assured that he hears your voice and will answer you.

My Heart's Cry to You, O Lord

Father, it's a new day, but I feel overwhelmed trying to untangle this complicated web of learning obstacles and behavioral challenges my child faces. Although I love my special-needs child, I sometimes wonder if I am up to the task of being an adequate caregiver. I believe that only you can equip me for today, the coming days, and the potential future difficulties. Please help me to remember that you have promised to meet my every need and that you alone are the master of transforming the most desperate situations into something beautiful. I trust you to redeem whatever suffering has taken place and restore all that was broken, battered, and bruised—for their good and your glory. Amen.

Deliver Us

1. "Listen to my prayer, O God, do not ignore my plea; hear me and answer me." This week, write down specific concerns you have for your family members. Then take the time to pray for each issue and write a verse alongside each problem. Next, pray these Scripture verses out loud, back to the Lord, with confidence that he hears you and will answer you.

2. "My thoughts trouble me and I am distraught. My heart is in anguish within me." Spend time locating Scripture verses on the peace of God. Write them down and refer to them several times each day to help calm yourself, despite any challenging or uncertain circumstances.

3. "Cast your cares on the Lord and he will sustain you; he will never let the righteous be shaken." During the coming week, be honest with God about your feelings of uncertainty and your lack of confidence to handle your child's special needs. Contact other parents who are dealing with similar challenges and seek out their counsel. Resist any natural tendency to go it alone in this vital parenting responsibility.

Out of the depths I cry to you, LORD;
Lord, hear my voice.
Let your ears be attentive
    to my cry for mercy.

If you, LORD, kept a record of sins,
    Lord, who could stand?
But with you there is forgiveness,
    so that we can, with reverence, serve you.

I wait for the LORD, my whole being waits,
    and in his word I put my hope.
I wait for the Lord
    more than watchmen wait for the morning,
    more than watchmen wait for the morning.

PSALM 130

CHAPTER 3

Dealing with Hurtful People

*If what we call love doesn't take us beyond
ourselves, it is not really love.*

Oswald Chambers

Marla didn't think she'd slept at all that night. From one lingering hour to the next, she had tossed and turned until she finally gave up altogether. She put on her robe and slippers and quietly slipped out of the bedroom so she didn't disturb her husband, Dean. Fifteen minutes later, she was sitting comfortably with a hot cup of coffee as she paged through her well-worn Bible. Flipping through the Psalms, one of Marla's favorite books, her eyes landed on Psalm 130. As she read it, she knew this was exactly what she needed right now:

> Out of the depths I cry to you, Lord;
> Lord, hear my voice.
> Let your ears be attentive
>   to my cry for mercy.

As Marla continued reading and then began to pray, she felt herself relax as the tension from the previous evening's conversation with Dean lost its vice grip on her emotions. Her stomach knotted and she felt sick as she recalled his words, because she realized she had blindly believed what he had said about his brother. She had lain in bed all night long wrestling with the thought that she should tell someone about Nick, maybe even the police.

But as the sunshine slowly began to infiltrate the kitchen, she realized she should have known better. After having been married to

Dean for so many years, she was usually wise enough to see through his constant criticism of Nick. Lately, Marla had begun to wonder if Dean acted like this because he was envious of Nick's success as a commercial realtor. On several occasions, she had tried to gently pursue this thought with Dean but to no avail. "That's ridiculous!" he responded most recently. "Are you saying I'm jealous of him? He's a loser! I'm not envious!" Marla quickly dropped the subject, but she continued to pray that Dean would take a much needed and long overdue look into his own heart issues concerning his only brother and his wife. But so far, as much as she was able to discern, nothing had changed.

Then last night, Dean had been so convincing, so amazingly persuasive, she started to believe him to the point that she thought Nick was involved in some corrupt business dealings with the city in order to land a huge account. Now, in the light of morning, she was embarrassed and ashamed of herself. She couldn't understand why she allowed Dean's resentment and bitterness against his brother to sway her like that. She knew it was no one's fault but her own that she actually believed him. She should have known better.

She sighed and gazed down at her coffee, wondering if Dean would ever be able to make amends with Nick and his wife. Marla certainly found it draining, and she was tired of Dean's constant ranting and how he allowed his anger toward others to distort the truth. "Help me, Lord," she prayed quietly. "Help us! Help him to love his brother and to love others. Help me to understand why Dean feels like this so I can be supportive and loving to him through all this. I don't see any other way to break through this impasse of bitterness and distrust."

She then looked up and saw the "Psalms" calendar next to the refrigerator and knew that she had turned to the only One who could help them.

> Out of the depths I cry to you, LORD;
> Lord, hear my voice. . . .
> I wait for the LORD, my whole being waits,
>   and in his word I put my hope.
> I wait for the Lord
>   more than watchmen wait for the morning,
>   more than watchmen wait for the morning.

Marla's sad experience is not uncommon. I've personally gone through similar scenarios on more occasions than I care to recall or admit. Unlike Marla, whose spouse is the one who harbors resentment and bitterness toward his brother and his brother's wife, I found myself on the listening end of an acquaintance who felt it was her obligation to inform me of a mutual business contact's questionable track record. Like Marla, I too endured some hours of inner unrest as I tried to unravel the real facts as opposed to the supposed facts I was given.

I later felt I had been duped—perhaps not intentionally, but duped nonetheless. I had walked right into a conversation trap I should have wisely avoided had I seen it coming. Instead, I found myself blindsided by a verbal assault against someone I didn't know very well, which meant that I had no idea if what was being said was true or not. But the person talking seemed credible and I ended up believing the slander. Eventually, just as Marla did, I began the work of repair in my own heart and mind toward the wrongly accused person. I asked the Lord to forgive me for not exiting that damaging conversation swiftly enough and for naively giving weight to the slanderer.

If there is one truly consistent principle in harboring bitterness and resentment against others, it is that the fallout from the disobedience of unforgiveness spreads far beyond the one offended. How can any of us cling to faults, injuries, and any number of real (or supposed) sins committed against us and not understand that we sabotage ourselves from the inside out? Jesus made this clear: "Forgive others as you have been forgiven." It's impossible for any of us to truly love another person if we keep tallying up their faults and slandering them in our hearts—or worse, to others.

May we all learn from Marla's experience and revelation, as well as my own. We are called first of all to forgive others of their offenses against us. Then we must learn to be discerning about what we hear from others. Finally, as Marla determined, we need to pray for reconciliation and the restoration of love. Together, let's purpose to put into practice this truth by Oswald Chambers: "If what we call love doesn't take us beyond ourselves, it is not really love."

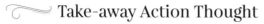

Take-away Action Thought

When you are tempted to listen to gossip and you begin to believe negative accounts about another person, swiftly step away from the conversation. Then prayerfully consider the source and make sure you're not participating in any type of slander or destructive communication. Seek to be a peacemaker and a rebuilder in every relationship as far as you are able.

My Heart's Cry to You, O Lord

Father, I am disappointed in myself. I unwisely allowed myself to get tangled up in a conversation where I sat listening to one embittered individual berate another. Please forgive me for not removing myself more quickly from this damaging conversation. And please help me to erase from my memory all the awful details I heard about that other person. I know better. I also realize that the person talking is angry and resentful. I should never listen to or believe any negative information from others, especially from a person who refuses to forgive. Amen.

Deliver Us

1. "If you, LORD, kept a record of sins, Lord, who could stand? But with you there is forgiveness." This week, spend a few minutes each day in introspective prayer. Ask the Lord to reveal to your heart anyone with whom you have a grievance. Then, if any individuals come to mind, prayerfully forgive them one by one and pray for them.

2. "I wait for the LORD, my whole being waits, and in his word I put my hope." During the next week, try to be more sensitive to

21

the conversations you're in. Ask the Lord to help you be more attentive and to listen better. If any of the conversations take a destructive turn, excuse yourself and walk away.

3. "I wait for the Lord more than watchmen wait for the morning, more than watchmen wait for the morning." During your quiet time, spend ten minutes silently waiting before the Lord. Remind yourself that God alone can transform broken people, troubled relationships, and the unforgiveness that festers within the human heart. Pray for each person in your life you know is struggling to forgive another.

I waited patiently for the LORD;
  he turned to me and heard my cry. . . .
 He put a new song in my mouth,
  a hymn of praise to our God.
Many will see and fear the LORD
  and put their trust in him. . . .

Many, LORD my God,
  are the wonders you have done,
  the things you planned for us.
None can compare with you;
  were I to speak and tell of your deeds,
  they would be too many to declare. . . .

Do not withhold your mercy from me, LORD;
  may your love and faithfulness always protect me. . . .

But as for me, I am poor and needy;
  may the Lord think of me.
You are my help and my deliverer;
  you are my God, do not delay.

PSALM 40

CHAPTER 4

Living Joyfully, Despite Chronic Health Issues

We wait and work. We wait and fight. We wait and conquer. We wait and proclaim. We wait and run. We wait and sacrifice. We wait and give. We wait and worship. Waiting on God is an action based on confident assurance of grace to come.

PAUL DAVID TRIPP

Recuperating from recent knee surgery, Natalie continued to enjoy her time at home until her surgeon cleared her to return to her nursing job at the medical clinic. While Natalie loved assisting patients, she felt the heavy toll that nursing had taken on her physically, and this surgery was just the latest physical challenge she had faced. Besides the bad knee, she suffered from ongoing and often debilitating thyroid problems and several autoimmune disorders that constantly flared up, leaving her exhausted and pain-ridden after a long day's work. Natalie's physician repeatedly cautioned her about doing too much. "But that goes along with the job description," Natalie countered. "It's my responsibility to help physically care for and transport patients from one bed to another, from one room to another."

On this particular morning, the sun was shining brightly and spring was right around the corner. The birds chirped as they flew from tree to tree, as if they too felt the welcome change in the air. Natalie longed to feel the same cheerful hope that all of nature seemed to be reveling in; and as she sat looking outside, she began to ponder her life.

She had always wanted to be a nurse. Even as a little girl, she pretended that her dolls and stuffed animals were patients with one ailment or another that needed treatment. The best gift she ever received was a toy medical kit with multiple instruments. Her friends had to join in and pretend to be sick patients, while they spent hours taking turns trying to cure the world of its diseases. Natalie smiled at those fond memories.

She knew she was blessed to have found her dream job a lot sooner than most folks do, and she was so grateful for the years of being able to work as a nursing professional. Who could have guessed that when she hit her thirties, her body would begin to revolt? First it was the thyroid issues and the months it took to tweak the right amount of medicine. Then an autoimmune disorder arose, followed by two more disorders within five years. She had done all she could to stay on top of her health challenges. But there were days when she wasn't sure how much longer she could keep working in the nursing field.

Not one to give up while there was still hope, Natalie had learned over the years to turn her attention to Scripture and prayer when she was in need of encouragement. Instead of starting yet another fruitless Internet search on her specific ailments in hopes of finding a new treatment or, better yet, a cure, Natalie knew her heart needed to be calmed and comforted most of all. So, being a woman of wisdom, Natalie opened up her Bible to the book of Psalms and found the words she needed especially at this moment:

> I waited patiently for the LORD;
>   he turned to me and heard my cry. . . .
>
> But as for me, I am poor and needy;
>   may the Lord think of me.
> You are my help and my deliverer;
>   you are my God, do not delay.

Who among us hasn't experienced a season or longer when our bodies seemingly turn against us, bringing us to a screeching halt through an accident, an illness, or a disease? Like Natalie, I experienced my share of ongoing pain after each of my shoulder surgeries and subsequent recoveries. Even now, many years later, I still battle chronic pain, and it is indeed wearisome. What I most appreciate about Natalie's story is that she worked hard to overcome her physical limitations and ailments through good daily care of herself. Equally important, she invested in her spiritual well-being with the same intentionality and intensity. Natalie understood that in order to be fit enough to endure the physical challenges we face in life we must be equally (or even more) fit spiritually.

As Natalie discovered, we need to dig deep into the treasure trove of Scripture, searching for God's life-giving and empowering promises. She managed to turn her focus away from her physical trials and tribulations, and turn instead to God. She made her top priority knowing who God is, how he has promised to be there with her, and how he has pledged to meet her every need.

She will attest to the fact that on any given day, her attitude and her quotient of hope vary in like measure to the time she spends with the Lord. As she recounted to me, "I find myself sharing the love of Jesus far more freely after I've spent time alone with the Lord." I, too, can attest to the same inner rejuvenation after investing in precious moments of solitude with Jesus. It makes all the difference in my day. It makes all the difference in how I respond to and receive whatever God brings to me. How about you?

Take-away Action Thought

When you start to feel weary or discouraged because of physical challenges, turn your focus to God and his promises to strengthen and sustain you as you take it day by day, and sometimes even hour by hour. Make sure to spend as much time caring for your spiritual well-being as you do for your body.

My Heart's Cry to You, O Lord

Father, this morning I awoke in such pain, I could hardly get out of bed. Then once I did get up, every part of my body ached. Please help me to lean all the more heavily on your promised grace and strength. Help me to discipline my mind to think only about this day and not allow worrisome thoughts about tomorrow to steal this day's joy. Give me a thankful heart and remind me to speak out my thanks to you aloud. I am indeed grateful. Never allow me to forget your many wonders and the blessings you constantly bestow on my life. Amen.

Deliver Us

1. "He put a new song in my mouth, a hymn of praise to our God." Each day this week, find a new hymn and meditate on the deep theological truth found in the lyrics. Then sing!

2. "Many, LORD my God, are the wonders you have done, the things you planned for us." Two evenings this week, spend time reflecting on the wonders God has accomplished on your behalf. Whether they are blessings seen or unseen, take the time to ponder God's goodness to you (all the time) and give thanks for his generous love toward you.

3. "Do not withhold your mercy from me, LORD; may your love and faithfulness always protect me." Search out seven promises in the Bible that speak of God's love and his faithfulness to his children (of which you are one!). Write them out on paper and each morning, at noon, and before bed, speak aloud these wonderful promises as a constant reminder to yourself that no matter what you face, God is with you.

Lord, how many are my foes!
    How many rise up against me!
Many are saying of me,
    "God will not deliver him."

But you, Lord, are a shield around me,
    my glory, the One who lifts my head high.
I call out to the Lord,
    and he answers me from his holy mountain.

I lie down and sleep;
    I wake again, because the Lord sustains me.
I will not fear though tens of thousands
    assail me on every side. . . .

From the Lord comes deliverance.
    May your blessing be on your people.

PSALM 3

CHAPTER 5

Being Purposeful, Despite Joblessness

It has been well said that no man ever sank under the burden of the day. It's when tomorrow's burden is added to the burden of today that the weight is more than a man can bear. Never load yourselves so, my friends. If you find yourselves so loaded, at least remember this: it is your own doing, not God's. He begs you to leave the future to Him and to mind the present.

GEORGE MACDONALD

Exhausted and longing for sleep, Nina often sat up in the middle of the night, poring over the employment ads and then submitting her résumé to every possible opening within a fifty-mile radius. Having been out of work for the past eighteen months, her bank account was diminishing at an alarming rate. It was getting so low, in fact, that she began to fret day and night over how much longer she would be able to pay her mortgage.

Before the company-wide layoffs, Nina had worked as an account manager for a computer sales company, whose IT programs were purchased by car dealerships across the country. Nina loved her job in part because she didn't need to travel very much since her territory was within driving distance of her home. But that all changed when the layoffs started and Nina was called on to handle multiple accounts in addition to her own.

Nina now saw that this had been the beginning of the end. She should have seen her own layoff coming sooner than she did. But thankfully, she had enough in her savings (and no debt other than her mortgage) to ride out this layoff. But it was becoming increasingly difficult to stay hopeful when no one seemed to be hiring in her area of expertise. It was almost as if the entire automotive industry was taking a step back, waiting to see when or if the economy would rebound.

No longer able to concentrate on job hunting so late into the night, Nina turned off her computer and moved to the living room. She retrieved a devotional book, her Bible, and her journal. As she began perusing the pages of her journal from recent weeks, she noticed a distressing theme that had been growing more ominous by the day: She had been losing her hope and her purpose. It was all there in black and white. She had been forcing herself to record her thoughts and feelings every day since her layoff, and she didn't like what she was reading. She knew it was hard to be off work, but couldn't she still live a purposeful life without being employed?

She then realized that she had just been moping around the house all these months, slowly descending into paralyzing despair. But she wasn't going to let herself succumb any further to this doom and gloom. Tomorrow, she was going to force herself to get out and find some meaningful volunteer position to serve in while she waited for God to open up her next job opportunity. She knew there had been increased need at the shelters and the food banks.

She had been too much in her own head these days. Surely there were others who had lost their jobs who were far worse off—people with families who couldn't pay their rent, people who didn't know where they would find their next meal. She may be able to help in some small way. While she knew she had a spiritual enemy who wanted her to stay paralyzed with depression, focused only on herself, she knew where to turn for help so that she could be a help to others.

> Lord, how many are my foes!
>   How many rise up against me! . . .

> From the Lord comes deliverance.
>   May your blessing be on your people.

When Nina shared with me how she recognized that spending so much time alone after her layoff had gotten her off track spiritually, mentally, and emotionally, I paused. Then I started to consider how often we all (even the gainfully employed among us) do this very same thing. Our life situations may be unique to us, but the results are often the same. Be it a job loss, grief, schism in a relationship, a grim diagnosis—whatever "it" is, too often we allow ourselves to lose our hope and purpose. Certainly, the stresses of life can take large tolls on us, and we all require ample time to rest and regroup. But I'm speaking of those subtle decisions, those tiny habitual choices we aren't even aware of that can blindside us with a spirit of fear or faithlessness. Worse still, we can lose our purpose for living.

For Christians, this should never be so. Our God is always in control, and whatever difficulties, challenges, and trials come our way are for our ultimate good and his glory. His word tells us that. So instead of allowing ourselves to become mired in what feels like a hopeless bog, we must take steps that will strengthen us from the inside out to face our trials and overcome them.

How? Let's take Nina's situation for example. She was up in the middle of the night searching for a job, with little to show for her efforts other than exhaustion the next day. She couldn't control the job market, and she knew it. What she could do, however, was to take her burdens to the Lord, pray for divine wisdom, help, and strength—and then leave those burdens with her faithful heavenly Father.

What's the next step? Nina wisely spent time reviewing her prayer journal, which alerted her to this downward spiral and her need to climb out of it through practical steps. She had been feeling paralyzed and purposeless, because she defined her life and her worth by her job description. When she lost that job, she lost her purpose and her own self-worth. Once she realized this, she began to look outward to others who were also suffering. Focusing on meeting the needs of others, while she waited on the Lord to open a new vocational door for her, gave Nina a new reason to get out of her own head and out of the house.

Like Nina, I've been in a similar position where I was so absorbed in trying to fix my situation that I lost my purpose and my hope, wondering what I was going to do tomorrow or the next day. May it stop now and never be so again! As George MacDonald so wisely said, "[God] begs you to leave the future to Him and to mind the present."

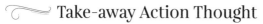 Take-away Action Thought

When you feel anxiety taking control of your emotions, spend more time with the Lord, poring over his powerful promises in Scripture, especially the Psalms. Write down all the verses you can find that speak of God as your perfect provider. Then find practical ways to step out and serve those in your life who may need you more than you realize.

My Heart's Cry to You, O Lord

Father, I am up again in the middle of the night, worrying and allowing my thoughts to linger in dark, scary places. Please help me to focus on you and to allow the promises I read in Scripture to renew my mind every single day. I need your faithful presence to protect me from my own wayward, sinful thoughts. Because I cannot fix what is out of my control, I find myself growing paralyzed and feeling purposeless. Lord, cover me with your loving-kindness and compassion, and help me to be self-disciplined to think faith-driven thoughts. I have choices to make every day about how I spend my time and what I choose to focus on. Let me wisely take my burdens to you and leave them in your care. Then give me the strength to go outside of myself and engage in ways to love and serve those around me. Amen.

Deliver Us

1. "Lord, how many are my foes! How many rise up against me!" This week, spend time each day writing down specific Bible passages that speak of God giving his children the courage they need

to face down their enemies. Meditate on these powerful verses each evening, knowing that your fearful, turbulent thoughts are often your most daunting enemies.

2. "I lie down and sleep; I wake again, because the LORD sustains me." Before bed each evening, spend time praising the Lord for every blessing he's given you in the past twenty-four hours. Then go to sleep contemplating his perfect provision for you.

3. "From the LORD comes deliverance." At noontime each day, locate a different Bible story in which God delivers someone from their foes. Then write down the specific enemies they faced and how Scripture tells us they felt during their trials. Then contemplate the goodness of God and how he always delivers his own.

God is our refuge and strength,
    an ever-present help in trouble.
Therefore we will not fear, though the earth give way
    and the mountains fall into the heart of the sea,
though its waters roar and foam
    and the mountains quake with their surging. . . .

Come and see what the LORD has done,
    the desolations he has brought on the earth.
He makes wars cease
    to the ends of the earth.
He breaks the bow and shatters the spear;
    he burns the shields with fire.
He says, "Be still, and know that I am God;
    I will be exalted among the nations,
    I will be exalted in the earth."

The LORD Almighty is with us;
    the God of Jacob is our fortress.

PSALM 46

CHAPTER 6

Surviving a Financial Crisis

*In time of trouble, say, "First, he brought me here. It is by
his will I am in this strait place; in that I will rest." Next, "He
will keep me here in his love, and give me grace in this trial
to behave as his child." Then say, "He will make the trial a
blessing, teaching me lessons he intends me to learn, and
working in me the grace he means to bestow." And last, say, "In
his good time he can bring me out again. How and when, he
knows." Therefore, say, "I am here (1) by God's appointment,
(2) in his keeping, (3) under his training, (4) for his time.*

ANDREW MURRAY

As Dan listened to his tax accountant explain the dire financial
condition of his family's car wash company, he threw up his
hands in disgust and despair. "I had no idea my brother hadn't
paid our taxes," Dan admitted honestly. "Jeff has always been in charge
of the business end of operations, and I handle the management of
the day-to-day responsibilities that keep the business up and running."
Shaking his head at the papers the accountant held out to him, Dan
was in shock. How could his brother have allowed this to happen?
How far in debt was their business? Why hadn't Jeff come to him?
Was there any way to dig out of this financial mess?

Dan took a deep breath and settled in for the duration of listening
to the hard-to-swallow summation of their once thriving business. As
the accountant handed him one report after another, Dan began to
understand where their finances had taken a turn for the worse. It was
pretty clear that after they expanded from three locations to six, they

took on too much debt too quickly. And then some of the machinery was installed incorrectly, which delayed new store openings by several weeks. But Jeff had told him they were fine. He assured him they had enough capital coming in from their other locations to make up the difference. Why did he lie? Why not tell Dan the truth?

Clearly, Dan wasn't going to receive any definitive answers about the hows and whys while sitting in this office. Standing up to leave, Dan thanked his accountant for delivering this devastating news personally and thoroughly. Armed with actual facts and figures, Dan knew that the most difficult conversation was yet to come. As he drove toward the main office to find his brother, conflicting thoughts and emotions overloaded his mind. He soon became so angry he couldn't even find the words. All he knew was that Jeff better have a good explanation for the mess he had gotten them into. But how could he ever trust him again? How could his own brother deceive him like this?

Pulling into the parking lot, he drove to a spot away from the building. He turned off the engine, took a deep breath, and began to pray. "Lord, calm me down. Help me not to say anything to Jeff that I'll regret. I'm angry with him, but I don't want to destroy our relationship. I honestly have no clue how this is going to work out. Help me, Lord, to trust in you for everything I'm going to need to do in the coming weeks and months. But first, help me to talk reasonably with Jeff and figure out our next step."

Then, as if in reply, Dan felt the powerful words of God's promise from Psalm 46 calm his battered soul.

> God is our refuge and strength,
> an ever-present help in trouble. . . .
>
> He makes wars cease
> to the ends of the earth. . . .
> He says, "Be still, and know that I am God;
> I will be exalted among the nations,
> I will be exalted in the earth."
>
> The LORD Almighty is with us;
> the God of Jacob is our fortress.

Certainly, Dan had a valid reason to confront his brother over his incompetent management of their family business. Because Dan had the black-and-white proof of what had transpired, Jeff could not deny the financial plight they were facing. While Dan had every right to ask the hard questions and get truthful answers from his brother, he can't get what he wants most: the ability to step back in time for a second chance to make different and more financially savvy choices.

As shocked and angry as he now felt, Dan understood that no matter what excuses or reasons Jeff might offer, this would not change the dismal hard facts. Their company was on the verge of bankruptcy. They owed tens of thousands of dollars to the IRS, plus penalties for late payments. And, perhaps most devastating of all, trust had been lost between the two brothers. So how should Dan respond to this emotional avalanche of unimaginable events?

Although he didn't realize it yet, Dan had already taken the first and most important step forward when he cried out to God. He turned his anger, pain, and disappointment in his brother into a heart-rending prayer. He instinctively understood that he himself wasn't wise enough, compassionate enough, or forgiving enough to respond in a way that would honor God and not destroy his relationship with his brother. He knew he needed the supernatural empowerment of the Holy Spirit to take the next step to resolve this financial family disaster and continue to work with Jeff.

As I contemplated the repercussions of this scenario, I wondered how I might respond in the same situation. Then I remembered that my husband and I did go through something similar many years ago. We had entrusted our investment funds to someone, and through a mistake made by our investor, we lost our money. When I look back at that devastating financial setback, I remember two things God immediately placed on our hearts and minds: (1) we needed to remember that everything belongs to God, and (2) we needed to fully forgive the person who lost our funds. Because of God's enabling grace, we were able to do both and move forward unencumbered by regret, anger, or bitterness. Praise the Lord for the grace to let go of especially hard losses, be they financial, relational, or any other kind.

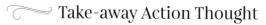 ## Take-away Action Thought

When you start to feel resentful or angry about your finances, remind yourself that everything you have is a blessing from God and everything belongs to him. If someone has hurt you, remember that forgiveness is nonnegotiable. Spend time in prayer asking the Lord to help you accept the situation, while determining your next steps to make up for what has been lost. Keep your accounts clear before the Lord so you're at peace. Be still and know that he is God!

My Heart's Cry to You, O Lord

Father, I am grieving this financial loss today. I never believed I cared that much about money, but having lost so much after working so hard has taken a toll on me. I'm waking up at night feeling anxious and afraid. I'm now distrustful of others because of one person's lies and deceitfulness. Help me, please, to place all my burdens into your faithful, capable hands. Then give me the grace to fully forgive this person who is responsible for my current pain and suffering. I need your divine wisdom to guide me in every area of my life. Most of all, I need to lay these weighty burdens at your feet and not keep picking them back up. I love you, Lord. I want to trust in your plan for my life, even when it doesn't seem to make sense. Amen.

Deliver Us

1. "God is our refuge and strength, an ever-present help in trouble." Each morning when you arise, spend time with the Lord, silently recounting his past faithfulness to you. Write down each

significant instance when you believed all was lost and then the Lord provided for you in spectacular and unexpected ways.

2. "Come and see what the Lord has done." Each evening this week, spend time worshiping the Lord by listening to (and singing) hymns of old with their rich theological truths. Close your eyes and meditate on them, and remind yourself that God is the same today and tomorrow and that you need not fear.

3. "Be still, and know that I am God; I will be exalted among the nations, I will be exalted in the earth." Write down practical steps you can take to demonstrate that you believe what you say about God's faithfulness. Do not give way to fear. Step out in faith, one day at a time, and be on the alert for God's good gifts every step of the way. Then share the blessings you observe with others to help build up their faith.

The LORD is my shepherd, I lack nothing.
    He makes me lie down in green pastures,
he leads me beside quiet waters,
    he refreshes my soul.
He guides me along the right paths
    for his name's sake.
Even though I walk
    through the darkest valley,
I will fear no evil,
    for you are with me;
your rod and your staff,
    they comfort me.

PSALM 23

CHAPTER 7

Finding Comfort in the Midst of Loneliness

*I've learned that in every circumstance that comes my
way, I can choose to respond in one of two ways: I can
whine—or I can worship! And I can't worship without giving
thanks. It just isn't possible. When we choose the pathway
of worship and giving thanks, especially in the midst of
difficult circumstances, there is a fragrance, a radiance, that
issues forth out of our lives to bless the Lord and others.*

Nancy Leigh DeMoss

Betsy drew in a deep breath on her way home from her sisters'
weekly Sunday meal. Having endured yet another kitchen
cleanup gripe session from Bonnie and Barb, Betsy felt relieved
to be free of her sisters' petty complaints about their husbands. She
realized she was still sensitive about certain topics ever since her own
husband, Craig, had passed away from a heart attack eighteen months
earlier. But really, Betsy thought to herself, didn't her sisters understand by now that she'd love to have a complaint about Craig? She
missed him so much—and their weekly grousing about all the little
things their husbands do or don't do was really getting to her. If they
only knew how she longed to hear Craig's car pull up to the house. If
only they understood how their words of complaint pierced her soul.

Betsy pulled into her driveway, hit the automatic garage door
opener, and slowly drove inside. Retrieving her empty casserole pan
and a few glass containers filled with leftovers the three sisters divided
among themselves each week, she went into the kitchen and put the

dishes in the refrigerator. Looking around her, she took stock of her surroundings. Everything was neat and clean, but it was far too quiet in this house. She wandered into the living room and picked up the book she was reading, trying to concentrate on it. But her thoughts kept straying back to her sisters' earlier conversation.

Both of her sisters were busy with their family's lives, and she felt like the odd woman out now. She knew she needed to start exploring new ways to invest in others' lives for their sake—and for her own. She wondered if it was time to dust off the dream that she and Craig had to become foster parents. They had almost completed all the requirements before Craig's health took a turn for the worse and he died. Although they were older than the average foster parents, they had passed every test they had to take. She knew Craig wouldn't want her sitting here by herself in this house. Alone and lonely. Not when she could be making a difference for a child who didn't have a stable, loving home life.

Excited now with this possibility, she prayed for the wisdom she needed to move forward. Then she went over to their desk and retrieved the file that had lain discarded for so many months after Craig's passing. Opening it up, she felt an unusual resurgence of hope. Yes, she believed it was indeed time to restart this dream. But before she did anything, she wanted to call Bonnie and Barb to fill them in. Maybe they'd be so excited for her that they'd stop their husband complaining. It could be a win-win for all of them.

As she reached for the phone, she noticed the lovely word picture of Psalm 23 that hung nearby. Her eyes fell on the verses that gave her the strength and even joy to go on.

> The Lord is my shepherd, I lack nothing.
>   He makes me lie down in green pastures,
> he leads me beside quiet waters,
>   he refreshes my soul.
> He guides me along the right paths
>   for his name's sake.

So much of what we experience in life is affected in large part (positively or negatively) by our perspective and attitude. Often, those around us don't realize that their words or actions add to our pain and suffering. Betsy realized her sisters were not intentionally trying to hurt her by lightheartedly grousing about their husbands. Rather, their comfortableness as sisters made them believe they could share honestly about what they were thinking or feeling on any given day or topic.

From Betsy's unique vantage point as a widow, her newfound sensitivity and awareness of the immenseness of losing a spouse gave her insight her sisters did not yet have. Wisely, she did make that conference call. After she shared her plans to revisit becoming a foster parent, she gently chastised her sisters for their poor attitudes and unkind words spoken about their respective spouses. Apologies were offered and accepted. Betsy was then able to share her struggles with suddenly finding herself a widow with little warning. Listening attentively, Bonnie and Barb promised to make themselves more available to her during the week when she felt most alone and lonely.

Perhaps the take-away lesson from this story is that Betsy didn't shy away from the Holy Spirit's nudging to communicate honestly with her sisters. Instead, she took the sometimes difficult (almost always uncomfortable) step of reaching out and speaking truthfully to her loved ones about their attitudes as well as her own. Together, they made a fresh commitment to speak and act with greater forethought and grace. She knew that if she did enter into the rewarding yet challenging world of foster parenting, she would definitely require the support of her two sisters. If we fast-forward the story here, we can see that she was successful with both her sisters and foster parenting. Betsy was no longer lonely—or alone.

⌒ Take-away Action Thought

When you feel lonely and alone, turn to the Lord and talk with him about what you're feeling. Then call a good friend or a family member and invite them to meet with you. Don't make the mistake of waiting for others to take the initiative. Step out and invite hospitality wherever you go.

My Heart's Cry to You, O Lord

Father, I am feeling alone and lonely today. I look at my calendar and, while it's not completely blank, I have too little time scheduled with those I love. Please help me to be open and honest with my family and friends about how I am feeling. They can't be expected to know what I am going through each day if I don't tell them. Give me the grace to step out even when I don't really feel like it and invite others to come over to my home. Help me to extend hospitality in a variety of ways so that I am a blessing to others. If there is a new opportunity you want me to venture into, please give me the wisdom to know how to proceed. No matter how I feel, Lord, I know that you promise to be with me and to never leave me. This truth alone comforts my soul deeply. Amen.

Deliver Us

1. "The Lord is my shepherd, I lack nothing." This week, write down every need you have in detail. Next to this list of needs, write down how God has met each one. Study these lists and then give thanks for God's perfect provision for you.

2. "He makes me lie down in green pastures, he leads me beside quiet waters, he refreshes my soul." Each evening this week, reflect on the day's events and bring to mind every blessing (small and large) that God has given you. Specifically reflect on those gifts from

God that refreshed and rejuvenated you. Then tell someone about what God did for you.

3. "He guides me along the right paths for his name's sake." Prayerfully review your life in its entirety and ask the Lord if he has something new he wants you to be involved in. Request the prayer support of several friends and family members to join with you during this season of seeking God's will for your life.

My God, my God, why have you forsaken me?
    Why are you so far from saving me,
        so far from my cries of anguish?
My God, I cry out by day, but you do not answer,
    by night, but I find no rest. . . .

In you our ancestors put their trust;
    they trusted and you delivered them.
To you they cried out and were saved;
    in you they trusted and were not put to shame. . . .

But you, Lord, do not be far from me.
    You are my strength; come quickly to help me. . . .

I will declare your name to my people;
    in the assembly I will praise you.
You who fear the Lord, praise him! . . .
All the ends of the earth
    will remember and turn to the Lord,
and all the families of the nations
    will bow down before him,
for dominion belongs to the Lord
    and he rules over the nations.

PSALM 22

CHAPTER 8

Making Peace with Unanswered Prayer

Gracious Lord, Thy name is love, in love receive my prayer.
Give me unwavering faith that supplications are never in
vain, that if I seem not to obtain my petitions I shall have
larger, richer answers, surpassing all that I ask or think.
Unsought, thou hast given me the greatest gift, the person
of thy Son, and in him thou wilt give me all I need.

PURITAN PRAYER

Cassie and Tim didn't know they were both carriers of Addison's disease (adrenal insufficiency syndrome)—until Ella was born. Within hours of her birth, she fell into distress, and the new parents soon became experts on dealing with their daughter's disease. When they learned they were expecting their third child, they were also told this baby had a 50 percent chance of being born with the same syndrome.

Now a toddler, Ella requires daily medications to make up the enzymes her body will never naturally produce. While she looks healthy, Cassie and Tim know that even a minor cold could be disastrous. They therefore keep a close watch on her, always keenly aware of any hint of an illness. Even though they pretty much know what to do by now, Cassie and Tim constantly feel as though they are on high alert with Ella's precarious health.

As Cassie neared her due date, she and Tim increased their prayers in both quantity and intensity. They would often watch their oldest child, Lee, playing with Ella and wonder what kind of life their new baby would be forced to live if born with this syndrome too. Although

Cassie tried not to be afraid, her racing heart sometimes woke her in the middle of the night. At that point, all she could do was pray that God would help her to let go of this fear of what might happen, to rest in his perfect provision, and to trust him to know what was best for her baby.

> But you, LORD, do not be far from me.
> You are my strength; come quickly to help me. . . .

The day finally arrived for the baby to be born. When she arrived at the hospital, Cassie explained Ella's syndrome to the attending nurses so they understood the risks her new baby might face immediately following delivery. Some ten hours later, Cassie gave birth to a perfectly beautiful baby girl whom they named Esther. Cradling her close, Cassie breathed out a sigh of gratefulness for the uneventful labor and delivery. All too soon, however, the nurse whisked baby Esther away for tests.

Within a few hours, Cassie and Tim received the difficult news that Esther had the same adrenal insufficiency syndrome. Unable to hold back the tears, Cassie held Esther tightly, softly whispering to her tiny daughter that she and Daddy would always make sure she had everything she needed to stay healthy and strong. Then she hoped that was a promise she could keep. With emotions running high, Cassie looked to Tim for the steadiness she needed from him, and she wasn't disappointed. Holding Cassie and Esther close, Tim said, "We knew God might have a different plan, Cassie. But we've done fine so far with Ella. We already know everything we need to know to parent a child with this syndrome. God knew that too. Let's trust him with the whys and be thankful for what he has given us."

> All the ends of the earth
> will remember and turn to the LORD,
> and all the families of the nations
> will bow down before him.

Raise your hand if you have prayed a prayer and God has yet to answer it. Raise your other hand if you have prayed a prayer and God answered it in a way that makes absolutely no sense to you. I'm sitting here in my office alternately raising both of my hands because I've been in both positions. And still, I continue to pray. In fact, I've learned over the years that when God answers a prayer differently than I had hoped or when I'm still waiting for an answer, I can be fully confident that God is doing something better than I can imagine.

But what about this story? How can giving birth to not just one but two children with a lifelong health challenge ever be good? From our human perspective, it can't. But then we aren't God. We can see life only in small measures, and we understand in limited ways. Our God never errs as he orchestrates both the minutia and the magnificent in our lives. He reigns supreme over humanity and all creation. God governs supreme over time as well. From our puny this-world-only perspective, we see so little. But God's vision encompasses a story larger than all time and space.

As we search through the Scriptures, we learn so much about his unchanging character, which when contemplated wisely should bring us immense comfort and security. He always does what is best for us and allows that which will bring him glory. No exceptions. So, while there will be countless prayers unanswered or answered differently than we had hoped, we continue to offer up our petitions fully assured that God hears our heart's every cry. Our task then is to make peace with the fact that on this side of heaven we will have unanswered questions. We won't always understand the mysterious ways that God works in our lives. And that's okay. We understand the important truth that he loved us enough to send his Son, Jesus, to die on the cross for our sins. If we accept that holy and perfect transaction, then we can rest assured we will spend eternity with our heavenly Father. And, really, that's all we need to know.

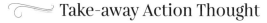 Take-away Action Thought

When you start to fret and fume about unanswered prayers, spend more time in prayer and ask the Lord to give you increased wisdom and understanding. Pray for a heart that is willing to humbly submit to whatever it is God has planned for your life.

My Heart's Cry to You, O Lord

Father, I am confused and disappointed that you didn't answer my prayers in the way I had hoped. I was so sure you would hear my heart's cry about this matter and then answer me accordingly. I believe in you and in your power to make the impossible possible. Why didn't you answer me as I asked? Please help me to accept your perfect will and to not give way to despair. I know that I am not in control; you are. Give me the grace I need to be content in whatever you deem best for me. Amen.

Deliver Us

1. "In you our ancestors put their trust; they trusted and you delivered them." Spend time this week looking at the lives of various biblical characters who trusted in the Lord to deliver them out of trouble. Then prayerfully remind yourself that God is the same yesterday, today, and tomorrow. If God helped deliver these men and women out of their trouble, he will deliver you.

2. "Do not be far from me, for trouble is near and there is no one to help." Each day this week, write down every concern or problem you're facing. Then look up specific Bible passages, especially in the Psalms, that bring you comfort for each challenging situation. Meditate on these promises in the sunlight of the day—and in the dark middle of the night when your worries wake you.

3. "You are my strength, come quickly to help me. I will declare your name to my people; in the assembly I will praise you." At the close of the week, spend time reflecting on how God met your every need and answered your prayers even if they were answered differently than you had hoped. If you feel confused or disappointed, place your trust in the knowledge that God always wants what is best for you.

I will praise you, LORD, with all my heart;
    before the "gods" I will sing your praise.
I will bow down toward your holy temple
    and will praise your name
        for your unfailing love and your faithfulness,
for you have so exalted your solemn decree
    that it surpasses your fame.
When I called, you answered me;
    you greatly emboldened me. . . .

Though I walk in the midst of trouble,
    you preserve my life.
You stretch out your hand against the anger of my foes;
    with your right hand you save me.
The LORD will vindicate me;
    your love, LORD, endures forever—
        do not abandon the works of your hands.

PSALM 138

CHAPTER 9

Living with Addiction

If we are to honor God by trusting Him, and if we are to find peace for ourselves, we must come to the place where we can honestly say, "God, I do not have to understand. I will just trust You."

JERRY BRIDGES

Maggie had a dream that night about the happy times the family had spent at the cottage when Jack was young. The dream was so vivid it felt real, looked real, and she could have sworn she even smelled the pine trees outside the cottage. Snuggled up comfortably in bed, a pulsing signal suddenly spoiled her dreamy peace. Unable to ignore her cell phone's insistent ringing, she turned on the light, got out of bed and stumbled across the room to answer it. It was 3:30 in the morning.

She was suddenly wide awake when she heard Jack on the line, sounding distraught. Maggie tried to clear her thoughts and make sense of what her son was saying. "Where are you, Jack?" she asked calmly even though she felt anything but calm.

"I'm still here at the center, but they're trying to hurt me. Mom, I'm scared. You have to come and get me now!" Then she lost him. Frozen to the spot, she looked at the number from which Jack had called: *Unknown.* Her mind started to reel with questions: Is Jack really in trouble? Is this another mental breakdown? Is he using again? Many more went through her mind as she prayed for God to show her what to do, how to pray.

Jack, who was now thirty-nine, had a long history of battling drug abuse and had experienced several mental breakdowns, so this bizarre call was nothing new to her. Over the years, his addictions had cost him his marriage, custody of his children, his business, and on more than one occasion nearly his life. Maggie had lost track of how many times she had received these SOS calls in the middle of the night that made her heart race. Every time he overdosed, emergency responders saved Jack's life with the use of Narcan to counteract the lethal drugs he had taken, followed by another episode in a series of rehabilitation stints.

The "before Maggie," as she liked to describe herself, would try to protect Jack from himself by checking up on him day and night, following him when his stories didn't add up, and even purchasing a safe to keep her valuables, money, and medications locked away from her out-of-control son whenever he visited. This "before Maggie" spent countless nights pacing the floor of her home, losing sleep, and feeling so exhausted day after day by the sheer drama Jack caused the family. Looking back, she considers it a miracle that the stress alone didn't cause her a heart attack. But that was all in the past.

The "after Maggie" who answered this most recent distress call has a completely different perspective—a perspective based on this formula: Quietness + Confidence = Strength. This "formula" comes from the passage in Isaiah 30:15 that says, "In quietness and confidence is your strength." Thinking long and hard on the truth of this verse, she found that the more she contemplated it, the more peace she experienced. For the first time since Jack had started using drugs, Maggie finally began getting a good night's sleep, because she chose to place her beloved but wayward son into the always capable (always on duty!) hands of her heavenly Father. Maggie realized it wasn't her battle to fight any longer, so she gave it to God.

> I will praise you, LORD, with all my heart;
>   before the "gods" I will sing your praise.

Instead of falling apart in despair over Jack, Maggie retreated from the uncontrollable into the steady and certain safety of God's promised sovereign care. Reading one verse after another in Psalm 138, Maggie's heart rate slowed and her breathing evened out. Slowly, all the inner chaos took a backseat to God's comforting truth. The "after Maggie" knew without a doubt that no human intervention could heal what was happening inside of Jack's broken heart, mind, and body. As much as she longed to rescue him from the path of self-destruction, the "after Maggie" knew that only God could work this kind of miracle.

Maggie also discovered that she now had greater confidence in God's purpose for herself as well as her son. She was no longer content to sit idly by and be overcome by anxiety. Instead, the "after Maggie" became a bold intercessor storming the gates of heaven on behalf of Jack, continuing to find her strength, resolve, and inner confidence in God alone. She knows that God always has been and always will be faithful to supply everything she needs as she prays for Jack. No matter what the circumstances, she has confidence in the faithfulness of God for herself and for her son.

Like Maggie, we too can learn over time to trust God with all that we don't understand—which is pretty much everything. We can develop the same spiritual muscles of faith, peace, and complete trust that Maggie did when she disciplined herself to spend time every day in God's word, allowing these powerful truths to percolate into her soul. None of us has to live as "before Christians" whose lives are characterized by tormenting fears. Rather, God wants his children to grow into "after" as robust, strong-hearted, stalwart truth-bearers who can face anything this life throws at us.

Take-away Action Thought

When you feel overwhelmed by anxiety because of what is happening in the lives of those you love, set yourself down before the God of heaven, open his word, and meditate long and hard on his faithful, life-giving promises.

My Heart's Cry to You, O Lord

Father, I want to honor you by trusting you completely every day, no matter how upset I may be in the moment. When I hear life-threatening news from those I hold most dear, my earnest desire is that I turn immediately to you for my comfort, my hope, and my peace. Help me to internalize the powerful and life-affirming promises that I read each day. Bring to my remembrance your words of truth so that I won't be found lacking in my faith, but armed and ready to do battle in prayer for my loved ones. Amen.

Deliver Us

1. "When I called, you answered me; you greatly emboldened me." When you feel tempted to spend your day worrying about the possible life-threatening struggles of your loved ones, spend time in prayer asking the Lord to give you the grace and the strength to pray with boldness and persistence. Never stop interceding for those you love.

2. "Though I walk in the midst of trouble, you preserve my life. You stretch out your hand against the anger of my foes; with your right hand you save me." Spend time each day this week journaling about specific instances when God preserved you and your loved ones. Go over each instance and give thanks for his constant care and faithfulness toward you—past, present, and future.

3. "The LORD will vindicate me; your love, LORD, endures forever— do not abandon the works of your hands." Daily this week, specifically pray these words from the psalm back to God. Plead with him to continue his good work in the lives of your loved ones. By doing so, you'll be shoring up your own hope in God's faithfulness.

Blessed is the one
    whose transgressions are forgiven,
    whose sins are covered.
Blessed is the one
    whose sin the LORD does not count against them
    and in whose spirit is no deceit.

When I kept silent,
    my bones wasted away
    through my groaning all day long.
For day and night
    your hand was heavy on me;
my strength was sapped
    as in the heat of summer.

Then I acknowledged my sin to you. . . .

And you forgave
    the guilt of my sin. . . .

Rejoice in the LORD and be glad, you righteous;
    sing, all you who are upright in heart!

PSALM 32

CHAPTER 10

Forgiving So We Can Move On

We're tempted to think that once we have forgiven someone, we're done. But forgiving someone is not just a past event. It's something we must continue to practice, even when we are dealing with an offense we have already forgiven. Even if I have forgiven you for something you have done in the past, I need to be careful that I don't slip into bitterness some time in the future. I need to keep practicing forgiveness every time I see you or think of you.

TIM LANE AND PAUL TRIPP

As Brad confirmed the reservations on his phone for tonight's dinner date with a woman he'd recently met, "nervous" didn't begin to describe the internal upheaval he felt. He hadn't had a first date like this for a long time; but it had been two years now since the divorce, and he knew he needed to move on with his life.

He felt sick inside, though, as he remembered how he had pleaded with Lisa to go to marital counseling with him. But she had already given up on their marriage and wasn't interested; long before she signed the divorce papers, it was obvious she was already in another relationship. That fact alone continued to eat away at Brad whenever he was reminded of how much that painful divorce had cost him personally. He vividly remembered how everything inside of him hurt for months after Lisa moved out. He could relate to those who said it was possible to die of a broken heart, because he felt he could do just that. Thank God for his friends and family who came around and stuck with him through those early terrible weeks and months.

Everyone who loved him gave him wise counsel, saying that he needed to forgive Lisa. They told him that although he wouldn't want to or feel like it, he wouldn't be free until he could forgive her and finally let her go. But he had found that a difficult pill to swallow. After all, he wasn't the one who had walked out. He had been trying to save their marriage. Yet he knew that his friends and family were right, and after a while by God's grace, he was able to forgive her. Still, whenever he was faced with a situation he wouldn't have been in if she hadn't ended the marriage, it was a struggle not to rehash everything she did to cause him such pain.

He knew, however, that he had to stop thinking that way. Shaking himself out of this unhealthy ruminating, Brad began to get ready for his evening out with someone else. At last he understood that new beginnings could begin only with forgiveness of the past. Lisa had hurt him—and she may continue to go on hurting others who loved her—but there was nothing he could or wanted to do about that. Although he most likely would never forget her, he knew he had truly forgiven her when that horrible weight was gone and he felt strong again.

> Rejoice in the LORD and be glad, you righteous;
> sing, all you who are upright in heart!

"Forgive us our sins as we forgive those who sin against us." These are the words Jesus gave his disciples when he taught them how to pray. But this one word—*forgiveness*— can be fraught and the act of forgiving seemingly impossible. Although the language is clear enough, we still tend to misunderstand what it means and why Jesus told us to do it. To forgive those who sin against us means that we, enabled by the Holy Spirit, offer full pardon to another person. It doesn't mean we will necessarily forget about the injury or the pain they caused us—nor does it mean that what they did wasn't wrong. There will be moments we will be reminded of what happened, like

Brad. The pivotal point arrives when we choose either to linger in those pain-filled memories or, as he wisely did, to release them and move on with our lives.

There's a reason why the apostle Paul tells the church in Philippi to think about "whatever is true, whatever is noble, whatever is right, whatever is pure, whatever is lovely, whatever is admirable—if anything is excellent or praiseworthy" (Phil. 4:8). God knows that what we think about determines who we become. Rather than give way to depressing, defeating, and demoralizing thoughts, we must "take captive every thought to make it obedient to Christ" (1 Cor. 10:5). We need to turn our minds to that which will build up our inner person in the grace and goodness of God. The Lord knows each of us will suffer at the hands of others. So, he put into place our immediate, go-to, run-to action plan: forgiveness. Plain and simple. When we are sinned against, we choose to forgive. Repeat. Repeat. Repeat. As we read in Luke 18:21–22,

> Then Peter came to Jesus and asked, "Lord, how many times shall I forgive my brother or sister who sins against me? Up to seven times?"
>
> Jesus answered, "I tell you, not seven times, but seventy-seven times."

As we obey God's desire for us to fully forgive (which is what Jesus meant here by "seventy-seven times"), he loads us up with his grace, compassion, and mercy. And who among us doesn't want more of these life-giving gifts? Instead of holing ourselves up with our enemy when we choose to not forgive, God sets into motion a supernatural freedom-embracing chain of transformation inside our hearts and minds. Let's choose to follow our Lord Jesus—who forgave even from the cross—and offer and receive forgiveness as easily as we breathe in and out. Then forgiveness can become the lifeblood of our physical, emotional, and spiritual bodies.

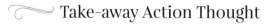 Take-away Action Thought

When you start to relive a grievance you have against someone you supposedly forgave, stop yourself. Instead, intentionally turn your thoughts to those things that are true, noble, right, pure, lovely, admirable, excellent, and praiseworthy.

My Heart's Cry to You, O Lord

Father, the last thing I expected this morning was to start feeling all the anger and bitterness I thought I had left behind. But I cannot place blame on anyone other than myself. I must take responsibility for how I allow my mind to indulge again in those past injuries. As soon as I thought about this wrong done to me, I should have taken that thought captive and refused to dwell in it. Please, Lord, help me to be swift to turn away from past injuries and pain. Give me the grace I need to entrust all that I am and everything I've endured into your righteous hands. I want to live free of anger and bitterness, but I realize that in order to do so I need to choose wisely every day of my life. Although I may never forget, I can choose to forgive and get on with living. Amen.

Deliver Us

1. "Blessed is the one whose transgressions are forgiven, whose sins are covered." Every morning this week, reflect on the many times the Lord has been so gracious to forgive you, remembering that Jesus died on the cross to save you and reconcile you to God. Spend time giving thanks to God for his mercy, compassion, and ongoing patience toward you.

2. "Then I acknowledged my sin to you and did not cover up my iniquity. I said, 'I will confess my transgressions to the Lord.'" Every evening this week, quietly reflect on your day. Ask the Lord

to reveal to you if you have intentionally, or even unintentionally, sinned against another person. If you discover you did so, ask for the Lord's forgiveness and then ask for forgiveness from the one you harmed.

3. "Rejoice in the LORD and be glad, you righteous; sing, all you who are upright in heart." Locate verses, especially in the Psalms, that speak about the Lord's mercy, compassion, and patience. Then write them out and read them each day as a reminder of God's faithful love toward you, no matter how many times you fall short of the mark.

My heart is not proud, LORD,
   my eyes are not haughty;
I do not concern myself with great matters
   or things too wonderful for me.
But I have calmed and quieted myself,
   I am like a weaned child with its mother;
   like a weaned child I am content.

Israel, put your hope in the LORD
   both now and forevermore.

PSALM 131

CHAPTER 11

Resting in God When Life Falls Apart

If I fail to choose gratitude, by default, I choose ingratitude. And once allowed into my life, ingratitude brings with it a lot of other undesirable companions that only succeed in tearing things up, then walking off with my joy. To not choose gratitude—daily and deliberately—is more costly than most realize.

NANCY LEIGH DEMOSS

Although she was busy with case files and calling the parents of her young clients from the school, Jill was feeling pretty anxious about who on the staff would receive notice that day about being laid off or let go by the management department. She felt sure, though, that she wasn't in either group. With so much to do on any given day, Jill couldn't imagine any scenario where her job was in jeopardy. She was already dealing with an overload of counseling clients who needed help.

Wrapping up her final call of the afternoon to the parent of one of the children with whom she met bimonthly in her office, she thought about this particular little girl's situation and how thankful Jill was to have the opportunity to bring some stability and healthy decision-making skills to her young life. It was really an honor and a privilege to be a voice in the lives of these children, given all the challenges they faced at home and at school.

Before Jill realized it, the workday had ended. She was just about to close her laptop when she realized she hadn't yet checked her email for the layoff update that had been promised. When she didn't see anything in her inbox, she thought that was pretty odd and decided to stop by her supervisor's office on her way out. Knocking on the glass door, Jill waited until Karen waved her in and told her to have a seat. For the first time, Jill began to feel nervous and braced herself.

"I'm sorry we didn't get a chance to talk earlier," Karen said. "And I'm sorry to tell you that yours was one of the positions that's been reduced to part time."

Stunned, Jill sat quietly for a minute before responding. "Well, I would be lying if I said I had expected this. With my current caseload, I don't have the time I need right now to see all my clients. What are the students going to do?"

"Well," Karen began, "it's not that you're not doing a wonderful job. You are. But the powers that be are cutting all across the board and, well, you're the most recent hire. Things may change in a few months, but as of next week, you've been reduced to three days a week."

Jill nodded and then stood up and walked out the door, saying a quiet goodbye as Karen watched her with sympathy. As she walked outside to the parking lot, she felt the grief welling up inside. She got into her car, put on her seatbelt, and began to sob. She didn't understand why this was happening. She loved her work. She loved the children. She was busier than she could manage in five days, let alone three. This didn't make any sense.

After a few minutes, when the sobbing stopped, she blew her nose and took a deep breath. She then focused on remembering how many times she had been at a loss about something that had happened or what she was going to do next, and yet the Lord had always helped her through it. He always took care of her. She therefore knew she would be all right now as well. Karen did say that it might just be temporary, but then again it may not. But still, something would come along. God had given Jill special abilities to be a blessing to others. Surely, he would provide new opportunities for her somewhere.

Instead of worrying or being angry, Jill decided to be grateful and hopeful. She took another deep breath and said aloud the verse she had read just that morning from Psalm 131:

> But I have calmed and quieted myself,
>   I am like a weaned child with its mother;
>   like a weaned child I am content.

The one certainty in life is its uncertainty, because we all know that life is always in motion. Like Jill, we must learn with every disappointment that God is still on his throne ruling with complete sovereign power. We need to believe that what he allows into our lives, he allows for our ultimate good and his glory—although it may not make sense at the time. Like Jill, when any of us receives distressing news, our immediate reaction is usually shock and disbelief. And that's understandable.

What matters next is that we step outside of our highly charged emotional response of the situation and turn toward the Lord. As we take a deep breath and exhale all of our pent-up disbelief, shock, and emotion over what has transpired, we can then begin the high and holy process of submitting to God's plan for us. And then? We give thanks and rest in him, calming and quieting ourselves in his loving presence. Once we lean in toward the Lord and allow the Holy Spirit to console and teach us, our hearts will be ready for the next step on the pathway to acceptance.

Despite our troubling circumstances, we can live contentedly today only if we turn to the Lord in humble trust and ask him to do for us what we are unable to do for ourselves. Our heart's cry may sound something like this: "Lord, I know you only want what is best for me, and even though I don't understand how this situation could ever be what is best, I will trust you. I will also obey you by giving thanks for what you are going to accomplish in and through me as I walk through this difficult season. Help me to embrace this difficulty with full confidence in you and enable me to live contently."

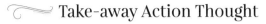 Take-away Action Thought

When you start to complain about whatever situation you're in today, ask for forgiveness and then start giving thanks for every single blessing in your life. Ask the Lord to clothe you with a spirit of humility and contentment, as you trust him to rule completely over your life in its entirety.

My Heart's Cry to You, O Lord

Father, this is the day you have made, and I will rejoice and be glad in it! Despite the challenging situation I find myself in, I will persevere in trusting you and put the full weight of my confidence in your perfect plan for my life. Please help me to lift up songs of praise to you each day. I know that you want only what is best for me. I have to trust in your ways and not in my own. Give me the grace I need to live in quiet contentment and not attempt to take over the reins of my life. I want my life to belong to you in its entirety. Amen.

Deliver Us

1. "My heart is not proud, Lord, my eyes are not haughty; I do not concern myself with great matters or things too wonderful for me." Every day this week, take a walk outside and silently consider and appreciate the grandeur of the natural world. Contemplate God's goodness to us, his beloved children, and how the natural world offers perspective and refreshment.

2. "But I have calmed and quieted myself, I am like a weaned child with its mother; like a weaned child I am content." After enjoying your daily walk outdoors, come inside and write out your thoughts. Make note of how you felt before you took your walk and how you feel afterward. Then write out a verse that describes your emotions for that day.

3. "Put your hope in the LORD both now and forevermore." Before bed each evening, pick a psalm and read it several times. As you read, ponder the depth and the richness of God's promises to you. Then offer up your thanks for his goodness to you and be content with what he gives.

The LORD is my rock, my fortress and my deliverer;
　　my God is my rock, in whom I take refuge,
　　my shield and the horn of my salvation, my stronghold.

I called to the LORD, who is worthy of praise,
　　and I have been saved from my enemies.
The cords of death entangled me;
　　the torrents of destruction overwhelmed me.
The cords of the grave coiled around me;
　　the snares of death confronted me.

In my distress I called to the LORD;
　　I cried to my God for help.
From his temple he heard my voice;
　　my cry came before him, into his ears. . . .

He reached down from on high and took hold of me;
　　he drew me out of deep waters.
He rescued me from my powerful enemy,
　　from my foes, who were too strong for me.

PSALM 18

CHAPTER 12

Staying Hopeful Though Life-Weary and Exhausted

If we are to trust God, we must learn to see that He is continuously at work in every aspect and every moment of our lives.

JERRY BRIDGES

Nora gratefully accepted the help of her kind neighbor as he made trip after trip outside, unloading the contents of her car and carrying them into her house. She felt badly that Jake was eating up his only day off helping her move back into her home, but she was still too weak from her hip surgery to offer any assistance—and, at age eighty-five, a bit too old. These days, Nora was getting used to asking for help and relying on neighbors, friends, and even strangers to help her.

She sat in her living room rocking chair, directing Jake box by box to whatever room her precious cargo needed to go. Unpacking these boxes would be for another day, she accepted resignedly. As she sat there, her mind began to wander back two months earlier when her son John had visited from across the state. It was supposed to be such a great solution to everyone's problems, but it ended up being a nightmare. Nothing had gone like she thought it would. Nothing.

When Nora found out that she needed another hip surgery, she balked. But her surgeon had been correct. "When you're in enough pain," he had said, "you'll be ready to have the surgery and get your hip repaired." She half-smiled remembering that correct prediction. When the pain grew so intense that sleeping in her bed became impossible, she scheduled her hip surgery and then contacted her son and her stepchildren to alert them. Nora sighed. It was at these moments that she wished her husband, Sam, was still alive. Sam knew how to communicate to her John and to Sam's own three kids far more effectively than she ever did.

Of course, after Nora called and explained her surgical procedure, including the estimated recovery time at home or in a rehabilitation center, all four adult children began making promises she knew from experience they wouldn't keep. Still, she graciously listened to John and her stepchildren assure her that they would be at the hospital for the surgery and would make sure one of them stayed with her for the next few weeks in her home. The following weeks leading up to Nora's surgery became a whirlwind of family arguments that almost made her want to cancel her surgery just to end the bickering as all four argued about who was going to do what for her!

On the day of the surgery, one of her stepsons was supposed to be at her house three hours prior to her scheduled check-in time, but he never showed up. She finally called a friend from church to take her and then stay during her procedure. No one called. No one visited. Not one of her four adult children even seemed to remember she was in the hospital. Only her friends kept vigil over her, faithfully visiting every day.

To Nora's surprise, John and his family arrived six weeks later to help pack her personal belongings and load them into a moving truck. Assuring her he would take care of all the details, John told his mom not to worry. Nora wondered for the first time since Sam had passed away if she might possibly be able to count on one of her adult children. So she did. But John's good nature and promises weren't to last. She soon discovered through her neighbors and friends that her house was up for sale—an estate sale no less! Nora was angry and shocked. She hadn't given her son or stepchildren permission to sell her home let alone all her possessions. When she confronted John, he became irate and called her an ungrateful old woman. Nora agreed with the old woman description, but ungrateful? Hardly.

Communication quickly deteriorated, and Nora knew she needed to go back home. But how? Her son said she was crazy and he refused to help her move, and her stepchildren agreed with John without knowing any of the facts. So, Nora called on those few close friends, who generously agreed to drive across the state and help her move back into her home. When they arrived at John's home, he knew better than to try and dissuade Nora any longer. Instead, John called her some abusive names and told her never wanted to see her again. Heartbroken and still weakened from her surgery, Nora cried silent tears most of the drive home.

While grieving over her family, she was grateful to have these dear friends—and she knew that the God who had taken care of her for eighty-five years would continue to take care of her until he called her home.

> In my distress I called to the LORD;
>   I cried to my God for help.
> From his temple he heard my voice;
>   my cry came before him, into his ears.

Nora was life-weary and exhausted. Who wouldn't be in her situation? At age eighty-five, she not only had to undergo major hip surgery, but her family further complicated her recovery with their unloving and selfish behavior. What the story above doesn't tell us is that Nora had raised her three stepchildren from elementary age forward after marrying their father, Sam. Nora's first husband had died in an automobile accident that had left her with a broken back and a broken heart. A few years later, Nora met Sam, and they combined their families to create a new lovingly blended one. Many years later, after Sam passed away, Nora's son John and her three stepchildren began coming around and demanding money from her. At every turn, they attempted to pressure her in an effort to wear her down to get what they wanted. For years, her adult children schemed to get control of her financial assets. No wonder she was life-weary and exhausted.

It doesn't matter if we are in a situation similar to Nora's or if we are facing an entirely different but equally trying set of circumstances. We all experience seasons when we feel life-weary and exhausted, no matter how old we are. We wonder if we have the strength to get up and face another day. But Nora learned from long experience that God was the One who would meet her every need. He promised to hear Nora's cries in the night and to protect her from her powerful enemies. And he did. As painful as it was to face, Nora couldn't rely on her family to support and help her. So she turned to the Lord, who provided for her through friends, neighbors, and even strangers. The point is that if we are to trust God we must, as Jerry Bridges writes, "learn to see that He is continuously at work in every aspect and every moment of our lives." Because he is. God is always working on our behalf. Always.

Isn't it just like the Lord to keep reminding us to go straight to him for our refuge and strength and protection? Reread the passages from Psalm 18 and count how many different ways God promises to come to our rescue. It's amazing. No matter how life-weary and exhausted we may feel, God's big-picture eternal plan will always reveal that he is close by, attending to our needs in ways we cannot begin to even fathom.

⟶ Take-away Action Thought

If you find yourself feeling life-weary and exhausted, turn your heart and mind to the Psalms to remind yourself that your help will always come from the Lord. God is your strength, your rock, your fortress, and your deliverer. You can take refuge in him until you are strong again. You can trust in him to protect you from even your most powerful enemies.

My Heart's Cry to You, O Lord

Father, I wonder if I've ever felt so tired. I feel beaten down and defeated. The saddest part is that those I love the most have been the ones to hurt me the most deeply. Please strengthen me, Lord. Help me to turn my eyes toward the heavens and wait patiently for help to come from your hand. I know that you hear my every cry and that you will protect me from even the most powerful enemies. But my broken heart, Lord, needs a special healing touch. Here I will sit and quietly wait for you to bestow your grace, your healing, and your hope into my soul once more. Amen.

Deliver Us

1. "The Lord is my rock, my fortress and my deliverer." Because you believe this, make a list of specific instances when he fulfilled these three promises to you. Reflect on each situation and how God moved in to make the difference between defeat and victory.

2. "My God is my rock, in whom I take refuge." Do a word search through the Psalms and make note of every verse that promises God as a refuge for those in trouble. Write out these verses in full and choose one to memorize this week.

3. "He reached down from on high and took told of me; he drew me out of deep waters. He rescued me from my powerful enemy." Close your eyes and picture this promise. Imagine how God can reach down and pluck you out of harm's way while he pushes your enemies far from you. Then spend time in prayer, asking God to help you recover your strength and find your purpose for living again, despite how weary you may be feeling right now.

Whoever dwells in the shelter of the Most High
　　will rest in the shadow of the Almighty.
I will say of the LORD, "He is my refuge and my fortress,
　　my God, in whom I trust." . . .

He will cover you with his feathers,
　　and under his wings you will find refuge;
　　his faithfulness will be your shield and rampart. . . .

"Because he loves me," says the LORD, "I will rescue him;
　　I will protect him, for he acknowledges my name.
He will call on me, and I will answer him;
　　I will be with him in trouble,
　　I will deliver him and honor him.
With long life I will satisfy him
　　and show him my salvation."

PSALM 91

CHAPTER 13

Finding Refuge in God
after Being Victimized

It will never be the depth of your love that causes you to forgive such heartless acts and attitudes. It will never be within your power to overlook the wicked lies and wild justifications of those who have made you distrustful of just about everybody. It will be—it can only be—the love of Christ transplanted into your believing heart that can exchange your weakness for His strength.

NANCY LEIGH DEMOSS

Kaylie and her twin brother, Kyle, had always been close. Some said it was because they had shared their mother's womb for nine months. Others, those who knew their sad family history, believed their unbreakable bond was a result of having only each other to rely on as they grew up. For as long as either Kaylie or Kyle could remember, their father was either physically absent or present and abusive. The twins' mother, Debbie, did her best to hold the family together despite the unpredictability and violent behavior of their father.

Debbie consistently worked two jobs, sometimes three when she could get the extra work. Their father would occasionally come home just long enough to eat all their food, make a mess of their rental house, and steal whatever cash Debbie had stashed away. He would then leave for weeks on end without telling anyone where he was going or how he managed to get by without working.

Kaylie and Kyle hated those afternoons when they got off the school bus and saw their father's beat-up truck in the driveway, because they knew that night there would be yelling, fighting, and sometimes even furniture thrown around as their parents argued. At a young age, the twins learned to stay out of their father's path when he was drinking. They would silently dart to the kitchen to grab something to eat before escaping to their rooms until bedtime.

While Debbie did her best to keep a roof over their heads and food on the table, that's where her parenting skills ended. Though she knew full well that her husband was a destructive influence on the twins, she continued to allow him to repeatedly reenter the home and wreak havoc on their lives by terrorizing them with threats of violence. It was the same pitiful pattern year after year. Only after their father had traumatized them did he leave again. And only after he left were Kaylie and Kyle able to take a deep breath and exhale. Both of them realized they could only count on each other for love and support.

This same sinful, dysfunctional pattern continued between their parents well into the twins' adulthood, and long after when Kaylie and Kyle had moved into lives and homes of their own. When Debbie was diagnosed with cancer and then died nine months later, this was the first time the twins had seen their father shaken and broken. They were gracious enough to include him in the funeral proceedings, but they wanted nothing to do with him after that.

Fast forward ten years later to breakfast at their favorite diner where Kyle was about to drop a bomb. "Dad contacted me about a year ago," he said to his sister. "We've been meeting every few weeks for lunch, and . . . and, well, he wants me to ask you to join us next time." Seeing her shocked face, he quickly added, "He's different, Kaylie. I promise."

"What do you mean he's 'different'? I thought we agreed we were better off never having to deal with him again. Have you forgotten what he did to us? To Mom?"

"I haven't forgotten, but I'm telling you he's changed and, well, he's dying. That's why he wants to see you, to see us both."

Kaylie had a hard time believing that their once abusive and violent father had truly changed. She could only think about the years of trauma they had endured at his hands. Kyle wasn't about to give up though. He had felt exactly the same way a year ago when their dad first contacted him and told him about his terminal illness. He too didn't believe their dad had changed, and he was even afraid of seeing him again. But Kyle also realized that their father needed their forgiveness. He even longed for it.

After more than an hour of this debate, Kyle said, "Kaylie, I've tried to persuade you that Dad is a different man. I've laid out every change I've seen with my own eyes. The only thing that we can do is pray about it. Maybe that's the first thing we should have done."

Looking at her brother, she saw in him all the love they had shared over the years. She finally realized that if Kyle was so sure, then she needed to take a chance and see for herself if their dad was really a different person now. "Okay," she said, "let's pray about it. Let's pray about giving him another chance."

Over the years, they had both found healing in the realization that they had a father in God himself. Maybe their heavenly Father had healed them, saved them, loved them to bring them now to the point of extending that healing, that forgiveness, that love to this sad and broken man who desperately needed it now more than ever before.

> Whoever dwells in the shelter of the Most High
>   will rest in the shadow of the Almighty.
> I will say of the LORD, "He is my refuge and my fortress,
>   my God, in whom I trust."

Sometimes, a lot of times, we tend to be cynical when it comes to believing that someone can truly change after years of being another way, especially if that person has hurt us. More often than not, I believe we get stuck in the emotions we experienced in times of suffering and trauma and will do anything to avoid going through such agony again. The positive aspect to remembering what happened in the past is that it can serve as protection in the future, but the negative aspect to dwelling on horrific events is that they can paralyze us with fear or anger. None of this honors the Lord or the love he calls us to exhibit toward others.

For those who have been victimized like Kaylie and Kyle, the natural human response is to shut out the perpetrator. But the supernatural response from the enabling of the Holy Spirit would be completely different if their father has indeed changed. Kyle, for his part, entered into a relationship with his father carefully, alertly, and prayerfully. What he discovered not only blessed his father but also set Kyle free from the anger and resentment he'd held on to for most of his life. And now, he wanted his beloved sister to experience the same inner freedom and reconciliation. Kyle remembering to pray about the situation was pivotal for them and for us.

Especially when facing hard situations, we need to pray first and ask for God's wisdom and discernment. We need to ask the Lord to make it perfectly clear if we should proceed. Whatever happens, we need to remain confident that God is our protector, our refuge, and our strong and mighty tower. Knowing that our God goes before us, we can rely on his abiding strength, grace, and courage as we enter situations that may very well be terrifying to us. We need to enter in wisely. But we should enter if indeed God is calling us to do so.

⌇ Take-away Action Thought

When you are faced with the difficult choice of entering into a situation that truly terrifies you, ask the Lord about it. Then seek out other mature believers for their wise counsel. Whatever you decide, place your full trust and confidence in God's perfect provision and protection for you.

My Heart's Cry to You, O Lord

Father, help me to know how to move forward in this situation that I never wanted or expected to be in. I'm not sure what is the best way to proceed, given all the past pain and suffering this person has caused me and others I love. I want to believe this person has changed. I pray it is so. And yet, even if they are different today, I'm still struggling with painful memories. I seem to be reliving all those awful events, and I feel agitated and anxious. Please help me to keep my thoughts on who you are, Lord. Never let me forget your precious love for me, your promise to protect and provide for me. Be with me now as I sit quietly in your presence seeking your direction. Amen.

Deliver Us

1. "He is my refuge and my fortress, my God, in whom I trust." Spend time looking up verses in the Psalms that contain the words *refuge* and *fortress*. Write them out in your journal and meditate on the power of these aspects of God's character and how each affects you.

2. "He will cover you with his feathers, and under his wings you will find refuge; his faithfulness will be your shield and rampart." This week, ask the Lord to help you recall specific times when he faithfully made a refuge for you when you were afraid or in trouble.

3. "He will call on me, and I will answer him; I will be with him in trouble, I will deliver him and honor him." Spend time each day looking up the stories of different Bible characters who were in trouble. Let God strengthen your heart as you read their stories of how he was faithful and delivered them.

In you, Lord, I have taken refuge;
  let me never be put to shame.
In your righteousness, rescue me and deliver me;
  turn your ear to me and save me.
Be my rock of refuge,
  to which I can always go;
give the command to save me,
  for you are my rock and my fortress. . . .

As for me, I will always have hope;
  I will praise you more and more.

My mouth will tell of your righteous deeds,
  of your saving acts all day long—
  though I know not how to relate them all. . . .

Since my youth, God, you have taught me,
  and to this day I declare your marvelous deeds.
Even when I am old and gray,
  do not forsake me, my God,
till I declare your power to the next generation,
  your mighty acts to all who are to come.

Your righteousness, God, reaches to the heavens,
  you who have done great things.

PSALM 71

CHAPTER 14

Grieving What Once Was

We are not necessarily doubting that God will do the best for us; we are wondering how painful the best will turn out to be.

C. S. Lewis

There are different types of grief. Some forms of grief you can see coming, because someone you love is critically ill and isn't going to recover. The second kind of grief blindsides you. You didn't see this coming and it leaves you reeling. Both versions of grief can hurt just as deeply and can throw us into an emotional tailspin before we realize what has happened. And what once was is no more and may never be again.

This week, I experienced both types of grief. In the first scenario, I had prior warning that the end was near. The second grief is still taking our world by storm as I write this, and each day I find myself off-kilter because of the dramatic changes we've had to make in our daily lives.

Back to the first grief scenario. When I heard last week from my cousin that his father (my favorite uncle from my childhood onward) was growing weaker from illness and old age, I realized that unless God gave my uncle some supernatural renewal of strength, we would be saying goodbye to him very soon. Yesterday, word arrived that he had passed away. Within hours, my cousin and his wife were on an airplane heading to his father's home states away from their own. While they were traveling, I prayed for my uncle's widow who would now be alone. I also prayed for our extended family, who have yet to know Jesus as Savior and Lord. I prayed that God's grace would comfort them during these next days, weeks, and months.

All through the week, I was reminiscing about the grand times I had enjoyed with my uncle, aunt, and cousins. My uncle was in the military so their family rarely stayed in any one city (state or country) longer than three years at a time, while my immediate family never moved. Our time together, therefore, was precious to us. It never seemed to matter how long a stretch there had been between our visits, we immediately meshed into one family at every reunion. These tender memories are bittersweet to me now, as I know we will never again have the opportunity to relive those happy times. Yet, despite the grief of losing him, the sweetness of our memories overshadows this temporary sadness.

Let's now address the second grief scenario, the one we never saw coming—the coronavirus pandemic. Since our country and much of the world has been practicing social distancing, I've been discovering much about myself and others close to me. I've slowly come to realize that I (along with almost everyone I know) have been grieving the loss of our "normal" lives in one way or another. This is a huge self-discovery for me. I've been chiding myself for feeling low and rebuking myself with words such as, "You're a Christian. You already know what's next. Why are you taking these changes and restrictions and ominous predictions so hard?" Now that I'm understanding more clearly the "why" of how I'm responding, I'm a lot more merciful toward myself. And I recognize that when there is loss of any kind, the normal and appropriate emotional response is to grieve.

But as C. S. Lewis said above, "We are not necessarily doubting that God will do the best for us; we are wondering how painful the best will turn out to be." Although right now we don't know what could be considered "best" in this time of worldwide upheaval and suffering, we have seen that as human activity was forced to a virtual standstill, the planet has had a chance to breathe—our pollution is dissipating and the waters are clearing. Some warring factions have made truces, and we have painfully discovered what is wrong with some of our systems that desperately need to be corrected. But maybe most importantly of all, many of us have come to realize what it is that we hold most dear—or, rather, who it is we hold most dear.

We live in interesting and frightening times. As I write this, none of us knows how long this will go on, nor do we know how the world will be different afterward. We only know that it won't be as it once was. Regardless of what happens, we can take comfort in knowing who it is that holds all our times in his gracious and loving hands.

> For you have been my hope, Sovereign LORD,
>   my confidence since my youth.
> From birth I have relied on you;
>   you brought me forth from my mother's womb.
>   I will ever praise you.

Grief and the grieving process are not to be dismissed lightly or ignored. No matter what type of loss we incur, the normal and appropriate emotional response is to mourn, which can take on identifiers such as sadness, denial, anger, or guilt. For me, I've discovered that when I'm mired in my grieving season (from either grief scenario), I crave a normal routine. I long for an ordinary day, and I pray for inner equilibrium, for calmness.

Over the past several weeks, which are turning into months at this point, our world has indeed been upended by this virus and our individual lives are no exception. So, what can we each do as we awaken to daily news feeds that depress rather than encourage? We create and then stick to a routine each and every day. Doubt me? Try it and see. As humans, we crave normalcy. We thrive on routine in the best of times, so why would we forfeit these small measures of comfort, these consoling habits in times of distress? I've determined that for myself, for as long as this season requires, I'm going to discipline myself to walk through each minute of each hour in quiet confidence in God, believing that he will give me the strength I require. I will continue to grieve, I'm sure. But while I'm dealing with my feelings, I'll be busy about my home doing as normal a routine as I can muster—and sometimes, as Elisabeth Elliot advises, just doing whatever is "the next thing."

∼ Take-away Action Thought

When your grief begins to overwhelm you, step away to a quiet place and contemplate the goodness of God. Commit your day to him and then try to create as normal a routine for yourself as possible while you're in this season of mourning. Place your full attention and effort into whatever your hand finds to do each moment of the day.

My Heart's Cry to You, O Lord

Father, I'm finally understanding how to best work through this grief I'm experiencing. I'm so thankful I can stop chastising myself because of how raw my emotions feel during this time of upheaval. Thank you, Lord, for bringing fresh insight as to how I can best manage these intense emotions. Now that I'm spending a portion of each day doing "normal" activities, I feel so much better. I suppose I never realized how much a creature of habit I was until my daily routines were threatened. But now I realize how wise it is for me to plan my day and then try to stick to that plan, working through my grief as I go about my day. I'm so grateful for ordinary days, Lord. May I never again take them for granted. Amen.

Deliver Us

1. "In your righteousness, rescue me and deliver me; turn your ear to me and save me." This week, pour out your grief to the Lord and look to the Psalms to find verses of comfort and encouragement. Allow your grief to have its expression, but don't let it drag you under emotionally. Meditate on the verses from the Psalms to remind yourself that grief is a normal and appropriate emotional response to loss.

2. "My mouth will tell of your righteous deeds, of your saving acts all day long." Each evening this week, plan your routine for the following day. Be purposeful in maintaining this routine to help you work through all your emotions of grief. Make sure you plan into each day a few normal activities that bring you comfort, hope, and encouragement.

3. "Your righteousness, God, reaches to the heavens, you who have done great things." Spend time contemplating the faithfulness of God in your life. Make a special effort to recall specific times and events when you felt lost and God brought a person, a message, or a provision that served as a reminder of his great love toward you.

May God be gracious to us and bless us
    and make his face shine on us—
so that your ways may be known on earth,
    your salvation among all nations.

May the peoples praise you, God;
    may all the peoples praise you.
May the nations be glad and sing for joy,
    for you rule the peoples with equity
    and guide the nations of the earth.
May the peoples praise you, God;
    may all the peoples praise you.

PSALM 67

CHAPTER 15

Thriving in Widowhood

Through suffering we become powerless so that we might reach the powerless. We like to serve from the power position. We'd rather be healthy, wealthy, and wise as we minister to the sick, poor, and ignorant. But people hear the gospel best when it comes from those who have known difficulty. If we preach God's Word yet have little personal familiarity with suffering, the credibility gap makes it difficult to speak into others' lives. But our suffering levels the playing field. The God-man who died on the cross is best shared with others by those who also carry a cross.

RANDY ALCORN

Lily awoke refreshed and ready to start her day. Always an early riser, she managed to accomplish more in the first few hours of her day than many folks did all day long. Her first priority, which was something she had practiced since her early years as a Christian, was to spend time alone with God. With her Bible, several daily devotionals, and her prayer journal, Lily tucked herself in under a blanket and began reading. She liked to mark up her Bible and other books, because she wanted to easily find again what she knew she would need in the future.

While Lily was methodical about her quiet times with the Lord, she was far more flexible with the remainder of her day. This was because she had learned a long time ago to hold lightly to her plans or pleasures in this world. She realized, from the things she had suffered, that the only true constant in life was God. So, being a wise woman, Lily made God her foundation and centerpiece. Everything else, she held with open hands, knowing she could put the full weight of her trust only in God's faithful plan.

After her quiet time, she turned to her computer to deal with the many emails in her inbox. Even though she was in her late seventies, she was happy to be technologically up to date. This turned out to be a real blessing for her and for many others, as it enabled her to run a ministry from her home to women like herself who had been widowed. When Lily's husband died some twenty years earlier, she had been forced to adjust to being single again long before she had expected it. But although she never remarried and lived alone all these years, she was never lonely.

Understanding too well the pain and grief of losing a spouse, Lily is able to empathize with and encourage newly widowed women. Lily listens with a tender compassion that comes from her own deep suffering. And in this way, she is able to help others look to God to touch their wounded hearts with his loving care and healing touch.

She has also made it her mission to spread hope, joy, and an eternal perspective to all who write to her seeking help. Over the years, her weekly electronic newsletter has expanded all across the country. Lily is pleased to think that, in a way, her own life seems to expand the older she grows. She credits God's ever-faithful watchfulness over her. Truly, his blessing and graciousness has shone upon her; and in turn, her light for Jesus shines all the brighter.

God, our God, blesses us.
May God bless us still.

When I heard Lily's beautiful story, I could only pray, "Lord, help me to learn to take all my personal disappointments, my lost dreams, my sorrow, my grief to you, my loving, always caring heavenly Father." Indeed, my prayer is that we would all choose as wisely as Lily did—that is, to hold life's blessings and gifts loosely, clinging tightly to God, confident that he is our only constant in this world. As we open ourselves freely to allow God to give and take as he sees best, he can then begin a precious transformation within our hearts so that we likewise may be a source of comfort, blessing, and encouragement to others.

While none of us seeks out suffering, in this broken world, it is unavoidable. We don't have to look far to see the heartache that touches those we love. What a blessed privilege it is, though, when we are given the opportunity to enter into another's pain and walk alongside them to a place of healing. What an honor to be called upon to lend a helping hand in times of trouble so that another may find it bearable.

May each of us, like Lily and countless others, submit to whatever form of suffering the Lord allows in our lives. May we, without angry accusations, trust that God is good and that he does good for our good.

⌒ Take-away Action Thought

When you feel the pain begin to drag you under emotionally, cry out to the Lord for help and deliverance. Wait on God to bring healing to your hurting soul. Confident that he will bring the help you need, prayerfully seek to encourage others who are also suffering in their own season of trials.

My Heart's Cry to You, O Lord

Father, I want to give you thanks for the compassionate way you hold me steady during my most vulnerable and grief-stricken moments. Even when my heart is broken, you give me hope. Help me always to be confident that in time my pain will lessen and that I will again find delight in living. Never did I imagine how you would use my suffering to be of help and encouragement to others who are hurting. Lord, you always do greater things than I can imagine. Thank you for being so tender in your nurturing of my soul. Your word brings me such comfort, such hope. My prayer today is that I can be a conduit of that same precious life-giving hope to others. Amen.

Deliver Us

1. "May God be gracious to us and bless us and make his face shine on us—so that your ways may be known on earth, your salvation among all the nations." This week, spend time reflecting on how God blessed you during your season of suffering. Make note in your journal of all the ways God has graciously provided for your needs: materially, emotionally, spiritually, and relationally.

2. "May the nations be glad and sing for joy, for you rule the peoples with equity and guide the nations of the earth." Using the list you made of God's blessings and provisions for you, deeply reflect on each individual gift and give credit to the Giver of all good gifts. Then spend time praying for whoever God has used so beautifully in your life. Finally, make it a point to share with each of these people how much of an impact they made on you during your time of need.

3. "May the peoples praise you, God; may all the peoples praise you." Set aside time to ask the Lord to reveal to you where you need to be giving back in service to others. Ask God to open up an opportunity for you to share the same encouragement and blessings you received from others. Make your desire to pass on the lessons you have learned and become a conduit of hope to others.

I will give thanks to you, Lord, with all my heart;
    I will tell of all your wonderful deeds.
I will be glad and rejoice in you;
    I will sing the praises of your name, O Most High. . . .

The Lord reigns forever;
    he has established his throne for judgment.
He rules the world in righteousness
    and judges the peoples with equity.
The Lord is a refuge for the oppressed,
    a stronghold in times of trouble.
Those who know your name trust in you,
    for you, Lord, have never forsaken those who seek you. . . .

But God will never forget the needy;
    the hope of the afflicted will never perish.
Arise, Lord, do not let mortals triumph;
    let the nations be judged in your presence.

PSALM 9

CHAPTER 16

Learning the Secret of Being Content

Gratitude, I'd say, is equally as contagious as its evil twin. If you're sick and tired of living in a home where all the joy and beauty has been sucked out through negative, unappreciative words and attitudes, you can make a change. You can become the kind of person you've always wanted to be around. The kind of person who makes Jesus and His gospel winsome to all who come within the reach of your grateful, "happy spirit." Two kinds of people: grateful and ungrateful. Worshipers and whiners.

Nancy Leigh DeMoss

Like most of us during this strange time of sheltering at home, I really needed to take a break from anything related to the coronavirus, especially since it was a Sunday evening. I had managed to finally turn my thoughts to a lovely book I was reading when my daughter came in with the news that the quarantine had been extended—again! I looked up at her and groaned. Again, like most of us, I was hoping against hope that we had already turned a corner fighting this illness. Then I groaned a second time because I had been happily immersed in something pleasant for a change, and my daughter's announcement brought back my dismal-at-best terrifying-at-worst thoughts of this virus. For a few blissful minutes, I had been feeling peaceful, rested, relaxed, unburdened, content— then *WHAM!*

I'm learning a great deal about myself in these uncertain days. For one thing, I've discovered how much I detest change of any kind. I tend to think that because I'm older now, I've pretty much figured out what works and what doesn't. And what doesn't work is focusing on what is wrong in the world instead of focusing on what is right where God is involved in his good work.

I'm also realizing that I have been making a personal idol of needing to understand all the hows and whys regarding the outbreak of this virus. I guess I consider it my "right" to know what can only be known and fully understood by God. So when I heard of this extended quarantine, my inner grumble exploded into outward groans. When I saw my daughter's shocked reaction, I was immediately convicted by my negative outburst.

I know she expects more of me, especially since I'm the one who continually challenges her to be thankful in *all* things and to refuse to grumble to God or to everyone else. No wonder she was unpleasantly surprised to hear me groan and grumble! It wasn't my finest mom moment to be sure.

But afterward, when I once again contemplated the repercussions of this longer quarantine, I started to see that in the midst of these uncertain times I still have the daily responsibility to behave as one of God's beloved children. And because I am that child, I must think, speak, and act in a way that brings glory and honor to him.

I have therefore made it my aim to stop grumbling—inwardly or outwardly—no matter how dire the news. Through God's enabling grace, I want to grow into a grumble-free me. I want to counter every negative thought, every dismal fact, every depressing statistic, with the eternal truth that God is alive and well and in full control—and that's all any of us needs to know. And when we remember this, then we can live an attitude of gratitude and sing praises to our heavenly Father, trusting him for today and tomorrow and always.

> I will give thanks to you, LORD, with all my heart;
>   I will tell of all your wonderful deeds.
> I will be glad and rejoice in you;
>   I will sing the praises of your name, O Most High.

In times of crisis, each of us struggles with our own inner battle against grumbling against God when life doesn't go as we planned or wanted. Instead, it is our duty as God's beloved children to conduct ourselves as those worthy of his name. This is especially important because people are watching us. If you are a person of faith, then those nearest and dearest to you are observing your every move and word. And if they've yet to take the step of faith toward God, you can be assured they are waiting to see how you are handling difficult times. In Philippians 2:14–16, the apostle Paul tells us exactly how to act:

> Do everything without grumbling or arguing, so that you may become blameless and pure, "children of God without fault in a warped and crooked generation." Then you will shine among them like stars in the sky as you hold firmly to the word of life.

Will we worship? Or will we whine? Will we give thanks to God? Or will we grumble and complain? If you're anything like me, the battle is real. But I so want to bring the honor and glory due to God by trusting him with all my questions—especially the whys. As we place the full weight of our trust into God's always powerful, loving hands, we can be at peace, at rest, we can relax, we can become unburdened, we can be content, just as Paul writes in Philippians 4:11–13:

> For I have learned to be content whatever the circumstances. I know what it is to be in need, and I know what it is to have plenty. I have learned the secret of being content in any and every situation, whether well fed or hungry, whether living in plenty or in want. I can do all this through him who gives me strength.

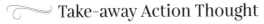 ## Take-away Action Thought

When you feel like grumbling, stop and remind yourself that you are really complaining against God. Whatever happens in your life, remember to pray about it and respond with a faith-awareness that even the hardest trials can be transformed into good by your all-loving God. Then you can step out of yourself and help others to also place their trust in him.

My Heart's Cry to You, O Lord

Father, I'm really struggling with my attitude and my words. I'm having such a difficult time accepting what is happening all around me. Such uncertainty alternately makes me upset and angry or afraid and anxious. None of these reactions is what you desire for me. You want me to trust you completely, even when I don't understand. You want me to learn to give thanks in all circumstances, because this is your will for me. Please help me to honor you by trusting you. Please help me to bring glory to your name by saying my thanks out loud and in public so that others will know what a faithful, loving God you are. Amen.

Deliver Us

1. "I will give thanks to you, LORD, with all my heart; I will tell of your wonderful deeds. I will be glad and rejoice in you; I will sing the praises of your name, O Most High." Each day this week, consider the good things God has done in your life and how he has blessed you when you felt discouraged. Then call a family member or friend and share one of these stories with them.

2. "The LORD is a refuge for the oppressed, a stronghold in times of trouble." Every evening, search out a psalm that speaks of God

being a refuge and a stronghold for his children. Write down these verses and carry them with you or post them someplace you'll easily see all day long.

3. "But God will never forget the needy; the hope of the afflicted will never perish." At mealtimes, remember to give thanks for the ongoing and new-every-morning blessings from the Lord. Be specific in your thanks so that others may be encouraged in their faith by the good work God has done for you and in you.

Keep me safe, my God,
for in you I take refuge.

I say to the LORD, "You are my Lord;
apart from you I have no good thing." . . .

LORD, you alone are my portion and my cup;
you make my lot secure.
The boundary lines have fallen for me in pleasant places;
surely I have a delightful inheritance.
I will praise the LORD, who counsels me;
even at night my heart instructs me.
I keep my eyes always on the LORD.
With him at my right hand, I will not be shaken.

PSALM 16

CHAPTER 17

Living as an Orphan

*If we are to trust God in adversity, we must use our minds
in those times to reason through the great truths of God's
sovereignty, wisdom, and love as they are revealed to us in
the Scriptures. We must not allow our emotions to hold sway
over our minds. . . . This does not mean we do not feel the pain
of adversity and heartache. . . . Nor does it mean we should
seek to bury our emotional pain in a stoic-like attitude. We are
meant to feel the pain of adversity, but we must resist allowing
that pain to cause us to lapse into hard thoughts about God.*

JERRY BRIDGES

Simon had just signed the papers that officially closed up his
father's estate. After this morning's final meeting, there was
nothing left for him to do in his role as the executor of his
parents' home and holdings. He drove away from the lawyer's office
feeling somewhat relieved that he had concluded all the legal minutia
his father had left behind after his death a few months earlier.

While Simon was grateful that the tedious task of sorting through
his parents' household was now complete, he was surprised at how
melancholic he suddenly felt. Being the last in his family line, he
recognized rather soberly that by definition, he was now an orphan.
True, as an adult man, Simon wasn't an orphan in the more common
sense of the word. But as a widower with no siblings and no children,
he suddenly felt very much alone in the world.

It had been just the two of them for so many years now that Simon
never stopped to think what life would be like after his dad was gone.
His mother had died fifteen years earlier, followed soon after by his

wife, Maggie. He and his father then figured out how to live as two men who, together, were growing older. Simon felt that they had accomplished that feat pretty well.

Now with his dad gone, Simon knew he needed to move forward with his life. But how? It seemed like ever since his mom's death and then Maggie's unexpected passing, he had just been circling around life taking care of his dad. Now that he was gone, Simon knew he had to start doing some things differently. But he honestly found it daunting. He had always had one of his parents to talk with about everything that mattered in life. When he married Maggie and she became part of the family, she was happy to live so close to his folks. Although they had expected children to come, it never happened.

Driving back home, Simon heard someone on his radio reading from Psalm 16. As he listened to the words and let them sink in, he knew he wasn't really alone—nor had he ever been alone. While he didn't know what was next for him, he knew he wanted the rest of his life to count for something bigger than himself.

> I say to the LORD, "You are my Lord;
>   apart from you I have no good thing." . . .
>
> Lord, you alone are my portion and my cup;
>   you make my lot secure.
> The boundary lines have fallen for me in pleasant places;
>   surely I have a delightful inheritance.

Most of us probably don't tend to think what it must feel like for someone to suddenly realize they are now an orphan. Although we may be adults, once we lose our parents, we are orphans nonetheless. It doesn't matter if they died at a ripe old age, it is still a huge loss for us. Some months ago, I heard a vibrant, gifted woman share how after her elderly mother's death, it stunned her to think that she was now really on her own.

As we know, life brings to all of us those heartbreaking moments when we say goodbye to those we love. It may be our parents or grandparents, or siblings, cousins, aunts, or uncles. Or we may be called on to endure the death of a child. Because we share an invisible bond, these relationships can hurt the most when torn asunder.

Imagine Simon's situation. As an only child, his last links to his family's past were severed when his father died. Afterward, he silently rebuked himself for not having asked more questions of his parents earlier. He no longer had any relatives who could fill in the gaps for him when he came across old photos of unrecognized people or mementos of unknown experiences, or if he needed to find out about important family medical history.

Certainly, all loss entails a season of grief and adjustment. Simon was blessed in being able to turn to the Lord in the midst of his sorrow and loss. He then beseeched the Lord for help and guidance as he took those first tenuous steps into the future on his own. Thankfully, he realized that although it hurt to lose those he loved, he was confident that as fellow believers, he and his family would reunite in the next life. But for now, Jesus' words from John 14:18 consoled him, "I will not leave you as orphans."

When his father was dying, Simon and he spent much time reading through the book of Psalms. In particular, Psalm 16:11 gave them both hope and comfort during those final weeks. May they also comfort us.

You make known to me the path of life;
    you will fill me with joy in your presence,
    with eternal pleasures at your right hand.

ᘒ Take-away Action Thought

When grief and sorrow overwhelm you, remember that you are never alone. God promises to be with you; and when that final moment in this life comes, you will be welcomed into eternity by Jesus.

My Heart's Cry to You, O Lord

Father, I am feeling alone and lonely these days. Never before have I been so aware of the fact that I am now an orphan. It's true that I have friends and neighbors and a church family. But none of these relationships replaces those I have lost through death. I miss my family members who have died, as well as those who shared life with me as part of our extended family. I am truly comforted knowing that I will be reunited with those who are fellow Christians. Yet, the honest truth is that I still mourn. Help me to spend quality time alone with you, Lord, every single day. Give me the strength to venture out and find creative ways to interact with others and serve those in my life right now. Revitalize my spirit, Lord, so that I am eager to minister to those who need me. Walk close by my side, Father, and help me to keep my eyes on you. Amen.

Deliver Us

1. "Keep me safe, my God, for in you I take refuge. I say to the LORD, 'You are my Lord; apart from you I have no good thing.'" Every day this week, set aside time in the morning and evening to meditate on the goodness of God in your life. With your journal in hand, write down every memory that comes to mind in which God protected you and provided for you.

2. "LORD, you alone are my portion and my cup; you make my lot secure." When you begin to feel overwhelmed by sorrow, turn to the book of Psalms. Begin reading Psalm 1 and continue reading psalm after psalm until you feel calm.

3. "I will praise the LORD, who counsels me; even at night my heart instructs me. I keep my eyes always on the LORD." If you awaken during the night and have to endure sleeplessness, turn on praise music (or play a song in your head), focusing your heart and mind on the words. Sing and praise the Lord through the night hours. Even if you don't feel it, remember that God is always close by and will meet your every need.

Trust in the LORD and do good;
    dwell in the land and enjoy safe pasture.
Take delight in the LORD,
    and he will give you the desires of your heart.

Commit your way to the LORD;
    trust in him and he will do this:
He will make your righteous reward shine like the dawn,
    your vindication like the noonday sun. . . .

Refrain from anger and turn from wrath;
    do not fret—it leads only to evil.
For those who are evil will be destroyed,
    but those who hope in the LORD will inherit the land. . . .

The mouths of the righteous utter wisdom,
    and their tongues speak what is just.
The law of their God is in their hearts;
    their feet do not slip.

PSALM 37

CHAPTER 18

Loving a Difficult Parent

*I know of no greater simplifier for all of life. What happens
is assigned. Does the intellect balk at that? Can we say that
there are things that happen to us that do not belong to our
lovingly assigned "portion"? Are some things, then, out of the
control of the Almighty? Every assignment is measured and
controlled for my eternal good. As I accept the given portion
other options are canceled. Decisions become much easier,
directions clearer, and hence my heart becomes inexpressibly
quieter. A quiet heart is content with what God gives.*

ELISABETH ELLIOT

"Your father may be having a heart attack. We are on our way to the hospital now. Meet us there." Brief. To the point. Devoid of any emotion. Yep, thought Tess, that's my mom.

Tess threw everything she could think of into her carryall for what would probably be another long day at the hospital. As she headed out the door, she practiced breathing in and out, in and out, until she felt calmer. She thought it was funny how those Lamaze breathing exercises from years ago when she was pregnant were still coming in handy today.

The morning had started off pleasantly enough with a peaceful cup of coffee, thinking about her day and all she needed to get done. But then the phone rang and she felt her shoulders tighten when she saw the Caller ID. "Not today," Tess had said aloud. "Please God, not today." After she hung up and began getting ready to head to the hospital, she began earnestly praying that her father would be all right, that this wasn't the end, not yet.

As Tess drove toward the hospital, she tried to keep at bay the one overarching fear that kept her awake too many nights: that her father would die before her mother. He was the only person who could keep her mom in check and Tess's only buffer from her constant criticism and negativity. "I don't want to lose him, Lord," she prayed. "I can't imagine how I'll handle taking care of Mom if Dad isn't around to run interference."

Then all her hurtful childhood memories began flooding her mind. She tried to stop them, but the reality that she could lose her father today overpowered any barriers she'd erected to protect herself. Even if he survived, she'd still have to spend the day with her mother. Although she'd forgiven her mom for how she treated her when she was growing up, Tess still felt a need to protect herself from her harshness, even now as an adult. And it wasn't just Tess who felt like that. Their entire extended family had their own personal war stories of when her mom had gone off on a rampage and everyone had to run for cover. The big question for Tess right now was how she could work through all this fallout from the past and stop being afraid of being with her today.

When she arrived at the hospital, Tess checked in at reception and then hurried up to the sixth floor where her father was being treated. On the way, she prayed that the Lord would help her to focus solely on meeting her dad's needs and for the grace to ignore any unkind comments her mom might say to her.

When Tess entered the room, she headed straight for his bed and grabbed his hand. "Dad, what happened? Mom said you may have had another heart attack. What do the doctors say?"

He smiled weakly as he held Tess's hands tightly. "They aren't sure yet. Someone is coming soon to take me down for more tests. I'm glad you're here, Honey."

Tess managed a smile and said, "Where else would I be, Dad? I love you!"

Once Tess could relax a bit, she looked up and saw her mom's face—and she braced herself for what she knew was coming.

"I was wondering when you were going to get here," she snipped. "Took your time, didn't you? Looks like you even put makeup on before leaving the house. Am I right? Isn't it more important to see your father without caring what you look like?"

Tess didn't answer. She turned back toward her father, who had heard every word. The compassion in his eyes told the whole story. "I'm here for you, Honey," they gently said to her.

Tess smiled again at him, knowing he understood. But in the back of her mind, she wondered, "Yes, but for how much longer, Dad? How much longer?" Then she remembered Psalm 37, and she found the comfort she needed as she held her elderly father's hand.

> Trust in the LORD and do good;
>   dwell in the land and enjoy safe pasture.
> Take delight in the LORD,
>   and he will give you the desires of your heart.
>
> Commit your way to the LORD;
>   trust in him and he will do this:
> He will make your righteous reward shine like the dawn,
>   your vindication like the noonday sun.
>
> Be still before the LORD
>   and wait patiently for him.

I wonder how many people, both men and women, can empathize with Tess's difficult relationship with her mother. Like too many adult children who struggle to maintain God-honoring and emotionally healthy relationships with their elderly parents, Tess had done the hard work of attempting to communicate her feelings to her mom. But to no avail. It was even worse for Tess since she was an only child and didn't have the support siblings might offer to help her (1) care for her elderly parents, or (2) provide emotional and spiritual support as she continued to love and serve her parents. Tess felt truly alone at times as she looked ahead into the future months and years—and what she pictured really scared her.

What Tess did know was that she was blessed with her own adult children, who loved her and understood how difficult Grandma could be. Tess also had close friends who had been through similar struggles with their own elderly parents, whose personalities and physical debilitation challenged their caregiving efforts on a daily basis. To listen to Tess talk, one could quickly see how little it took to send her spiraling into a dark emotional place when it concerned her mom. Admittedly, Tess's mother was not loving, kind, or appreciative of anything Tess did for her. So it was completely understandable that Tess dreaded the thought that her father would die before her mother and that Tess would be left caring for this person who was about as un-motherly as a woman could be.

As Tess sat with her dad that day in the hospital, a window of opportunity allowed her to be alone with him while her mother went to get lunch in the cafeteria. After her mom had left the room, Tess's dad said exactly what she needed to hear. "Tess, I know what you fear most in the world, and I understand why. But if God takes me home before your mom, I am confident that the Lord will give you everything you need to care for her. Never doubt God's plans or his provision. It won't be easy, but we know that if God calls us to a task, he gives us the strength and the grace to see it through to the end. I love you, Honey. Never forget that."

When he passed away a year later, Tess still remembered his comforting words on that long day in the hospital. Although from a human perspective, Tess's worst nightmare did come to pass when her dad died before her mom, God had done something remarkable inside of Tess. She had grown and matured in ways she never expected. Her difficult situation with her mom didn't change, but God indeed faithfully supplied Tess with exactly what she needed—one day at a time—in order to care for her hard-to-please mother. Perhaps what surprised Tess most was that her fears were gone, because the Lord's enabling power helped her to face what she believed was the worst. She is surviving, and on most days, Tess would even say she is thriving.

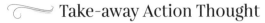

Take-away Action Thought

When you begin to worry that you won't have the strength to fulfill the task the Lord has placed before you, especially in dealing with a difficult parent or another relation, stop those faithless thoughts dead in their tracks. Then pick a psalm like Psalm 37 and read it aloud to yourself until you are once again confident that God truly does provide everything you need to get through this, one day at a time.

My Heart's Cry to You, O Lord

Father, you already know what I'm thinking and what I'm feeling. I'm frightened, Lord. I'm scared of what my life will be like if the parent I'm closest to dies before the one I struggle with does. I feel bad even admitting to you how often I feel my heart race when I consider what might happen. Help me to keep my focus solely on you, Lord. Help me to be confident in your strength and your grace, not my own. I'm not strong enough to handle this challenge in my own power. Please help me to rest in you day and night; and come what may, give me the wisdom and the grace to accept the hard assignments you have for me in loving those who are unlovable. Amen.

Deliver Us

1. "Trust in the LORD and do good; dwell in the land and enjoy safe pasture." Today, spend time in prayer, asking God to help you to trust him with all your todays and all your tomorrows. Then ask him to help you discover creative ways to do good to your parents.

2. "Commit your way to the LORD; trust in him and he will do this." In your journal, write down specific instances when you saw God do a transforming work in you so that you were able to serve others well. Perhaps it was by gracing you with an unnatural

calmness, or maybe it was by orchestrating help from a friend. In any case, spend time calling to mind God's faithfulness to you and thank him for it.

3. "Refrain from anger and turn from wrath; do not fret—it leads only to evil." Sitting before the Lord, pray for him to reveal any areas of unforgiveness or bitterness you may be harboring in your heart. Figuratively hand over to God any unforgiven offenses, and then leave them in his faithful and righteous hands.

Blessed are those who have regard for the weak;
    the LORD delivers them in times of trouble.
The LORD protects and preserves them—
    they are counted among the blessed in the land—
    he does not give them over to the desire of their foes.
The LORD sustains them on their sickbed
    and restores them from their bed of illness. . . .

I know that you are pleased with me,
    for my enemy does not triumph over me.
Because of my integrity you uphold me
    and set me in your presence forever.

Praise be to the LORD, the God of Israel,
    from everlasting to everlasting.

PSALM 41

CHAPTER 19

Finding Strength in Weakness

We come into this world needy, and we leave it the same way.
Without suffering we would forget our neediness. If suffering
seems too high a price for faith, it's because we underestimate
faith's value. Suffering uncovers our trust in God-substitutes
and declares our need to transfer our trust to the only One who
can bear its weight. God uses suffering to bring us to the end
of ourselves and back to Christ. And that is worth any cost.

RANDY ALCORN

When seventy-five-year-old Becky offered to take care of her neighbor's two little girls, Renee and Ruth, after school each day, she hardly expected to be fighting breast cancer at the same time.

She had been shocked when her doctor ordered a mammogram following her annual check-up. Several extensive scans and a painful biopsy later, Becky was told she had breast cancer. The cancer was still in the early stages, so that was the good news. After the lumpectomy, Becky went through weeks of radiation treatments, which left her exhausted—though she was grateful to be spared from chemotherapy. While she was glad to be done with her daily treatments, she missed the cheerful nurses who had helped her get through it all with their encouragement and beautiful smiles. Becky promised to come back to the hospital with some of her much-talked-about homemade cinnamon rolls—but only after she began to feel better and regain some strength.

Right now, her energy levels were still battling their way back into existence. Becky had never felt so worn out and exhausted before.

Ever. She realized her age had a lot to do with how quickly (or slowly) her body would regain its former strength. But she had promised her next-door neighbor, Cindy, that she would watch her little girls while Cindy went to work in the late afternoons at the high school. Cindy was a single mom who didn't make much money, so she really needed someone like Becky to watch the girls every day until 5:30 when she came home.

Becky had been the answer to Cindy's prayer—and little Renee and Ruth were also the answer to Becky's prayers. After her daughter's family moved across the country for a job relocation, Becky felt so alone and began praying for God to connect her with another family to love and serve since she couldn't be with hers now. Then Cindy moved in next door and a whole new chapter opened up in Becky's life. She was delighted to have this babysitting job and was looking forward to it when she got the bad news from her doctor.

But Becky was a woman of faith and knew that God would work it all out somehow. She needed Renee and Ruth—and Cindy—in her life, and they needed Becky. As Paul wrote in his second letter to the Corinthian church, Becky knew that God's grace was also sufficient for her, because his "power is made perfect in weakness," and that when she was weak, then she was strong. Although she was exhausted and needed to rest, she was confident that God would give her the strength in her weakness to be a blessing for her neighbors and to herself.

> Blessed are those who have regard for the weak;
>   the LORD delivers them in times of trouble.
> The LORD protects and preserves them. . . .
> The LORD sustains them on their sickbed
>   and restores them from their bed of illness.

Exhaustion is a terrible taskmaster. Whether we are recovering from a life-threatening diagnosis such as cancer, or we are simply spent from having overworked and overextended ourselves, exhaustion makes everything seem impossible. This is why it is best to not over-think or overexert ourselves when we are overly tired or in a physically weakened state. In fact, God wants us to listen to what our bodies are telling us and then do what's right: rest.

God encourages us to rest our weary, weak selves in him. He wants to take care of us. Although we may not understand why we're going through something hard, we should remember that he can use our pain and suffering in whatever form it comes to us (physical, emotional, relational, vocational, financial, etc.) to draw us closer to him. As we do this, we remember that we are completely dependent on our loving heavenly Father.

It's too bad that we tend to fight against the common sense God has given us and try to push through the pain, when God may very well be inviting us into a place of trustful rest. Sometimes God allows the intersection of what we promised we would do with what we are actually able to do. Sometimes God is trying to get our attention long enough so that we turn to him in humble, willing dependence—fi-nally realizing that when we are weak, that is when we just may be at our strongest. Isn't that the best place of all to be?

Take-away Action Thought

When you feel so exhausted that everything seems impossible, step away from the worry and the overthinking and rest. Then after you've rested, ask God to show you the next step to take, know-ing that sometimes he may want you to step away from service for a time.

My Heart's Cry to You, O Lord

Father, I woke up this morning feeling no stronger than yesterday. I felt, if anything, more discouraged. I so hoped that by now I would have regained my stamina. I have made commitments to help others, and they are depending on me. Please give me the wisdom I need to know if (and when) I'm strong enough to start serving again. You know that my heart longs for me to be up and around, busy with life once more. But I also realize that I am fully dependent on you and must submit myself to your perfect plan, your timing, and your purpose for me. Amen.

Deliver Us

1. "The LORD sustains them on their sickbed and restores them from their bed of illness." Each morning this week, spend time reading through the book of Psalms and allow the encouragement of God to uplift your heart and soul. Ask the Lord to help you to be patient while your body recovers. While you're resting, find specific blessings for which you're grateful and then give thanks all the day long.

2. "I know that you are pleased with me, for my enemy does not triumph over me." If you start to fall into false guilt about not being able to serve as you once did, you need to stop these unbiblical thoughts. Remind yourself that by resting, you are submitting to God's plan and that the Lord knows your heart's desire to get back to serving.

3. "Because of my integrity you uphold me and set me in your presence forever." Each evening this week, open your journal and prayerfully begin writing down the names of those with whom you would normally interact or serve. While you're recuperating, contact these individuals and ask them how you can pray specifically for them. Find your comfort in knowing that although you may not be physically strong enough to serve, you can always pray.

In you, LORD my God,
    I put my trust. . . .

No one who hopes in you
    will ever be put to shame,
but shame will come on those
    who are treacherous without cause.

Show me your ways, LORD,
    teach me your paths.
Guide me in your truth and teach me,
    for you are God my Savior,
    and my hope is in you all day long. . . .

Turn to me and be gracious to me,
    for I am lonely and afflicted.
Relieve the troubles of my heart
    and free me from my anguish. . . .

Guard my life and rescue me;
    do not let me be put to shame,
    for I take refuge in you.
May integrity and uprightness protect me,
    because my hope, LORD, is in you.

PSALM 25

CHAPTER 20

Hoping in God's Love for Unbelievers

*Real, sturdy, lasting peace, peace that doesn't rise and fall
with circumstances, isn't to be found in picking apart your
life until you have understood all of the components. You
will never understand it all because God, for your good and
his glory, keeps some of it shrouded in mystery. So peace
is found only in trust, trust in the One who is in careful
control of all the things that tend to rob you of your peace.*

PAUL DAVID TRIPP

It was early morning and Lydia was out power walking, trying to
release the stress she was still feeling from the previous evening.
What in the world was Trish thinking? How could she believe that
forcing a reconciliation between Sally and Lydia would work? Lydia
could have told Trish what would happen, if only Trish had thought
to ask her about it first. But she didn't, and now Lydia could only pray
about how she could try to repair the damage. She needed God's help
to understand what she needed to do next.

When Lydia completed her customary three-mile loop around
the path that ended at her street, she felt physically drained but still
wound up emotionally. As she showered and got ready for her day,
she couldn't get last night out of her head. It was all she could do to
keep from breaking down into a weeping mess, which she didn't want
to do just before she had to go to work. She would never forget the
shocked and furious look on Sally's face when Lydia had walked in
the door of the restaurant, giving a whole new meaning to "surprise
party." Why did Lydia believe Trish when she told her that Sally had

made other plans this year for their joint birthday, and that it would just be Lydia and Trish at the restaurant? The twins always celebrated their birthday together. It was Mom that Sally didn't want there.

Until last night, Lydia had been respectful of abiding by Sally's wishes of not making contact until Sally was ready to talk again. Sally, an agnostic, was furious when her mother told her she had become a Christian. Sally had made it perfectly clear that unless her mom retracted her faith, she didn't want to see her.

This, of course, broke Lydia's heart. While Trish wasn't a believer either, at least she wasn't hostile about Christianity and she still wanted to have a relationship with her mother. All Lydia could do was pray for both of her daughters to come to the same saving faith she had found. So that's what she did and will continue to do: ask the Lord to reopen the door that at the present moment appears nailed shut.

> Show me your ways, LORD,
>   teach me your paths.
> Guide me in your truth and teach me,
>   for you are God my Savior,
>   and my hope is in you all day long.

Lydia's deepest desire was for both of her daughters to come to faith in Jesus. She handled the rejection from Sally like a trooper and didn't give way to fear or anger. She could have done both, given her Sally's angry dismissal of her newfound faith. Instead, Lydia removed herself from the situation and labored harder than ever in prayer. Lydia was (and is) trusting that God will soften her girls' hearts over time. She hopes to win them over in love, one act of service at a time, one selfless conversation at a time.

Imagine her dismay at finding herself in a situation she didn't create that resulted in putting her more at odds than ever with Sally. She reeled from this well-intentioned but disastrous plan to reconcile her and Sally. Lydia couldn't blame Trish for wanting the three of them to be close again, especially on her and Sally's birthday, to have the same relationship they had before Lydia became a believer. Nor did Lydia feel a sense of hopelessness from Sally's harsh reaction.

Lydia wisely understands that while she may not have the answers her heart is longing to know, she must silence the voices of her internal enemies of despair and defeat. She knows that no matter what the situation, no matter how little she knows about finding a remedy, she can still grow in her faith through it. Lydia therefore thinks of this time as being in between what once was and what may be. While she continues to love both her daughters and hopefully be a good witness of her faith to them, for now she is calling this her personal "growing season." She has made it her daily purpose to grow to know God better. To lean in more closely to what his word says about impossible situations. And to allow his precious promises of faithfulness to cover her, body and soul. It's all she can do. It's all God expects her to do.

⌒ Take-away Action Thought

When you feel as though everything is upside down, retreat to God's word and meditate long and hard on his promises of enduring faithfulness, especially in the Psalms. Meditate on these encouraging verses and commit them to memory.

My Heart's Cry to You, O Lord

Father, please help me to lean into your word during these next weeks. I know how easy it is for me to fall into discouragement and become depressed when I linger too long thinking about the unbelief of those I love most. Help me to put my trust in the good work I know you are doing in me and in my life. I need to keep my focus on your promises of enduring faithfulness, not on what I can see with my eyes. You are the God of the impossible. I believe this truth with all of my heart. Please help me to grow strong in the strength of your might.

Help me to remember that I don't need to understand everything that is happening. I only need to know that you know. Amen.

Deliver Us

1. "In you, LORD my God, I put my trust. I trust in you; do not let me be put to shame, nor let my enemies triumph over me." Every morning when you get up, spend time meditating on God's enduring faithfulness. Carry verses with you throughout the day to look at and be encouraged. Your enemies are not other people. Your enemies are your own faithless thoughts and fears. Trust God to overcome all your doubts.

2. "Guide me in your truth and teach me, for you are God my Savior, and my hope is in you all day long." Write down in your journal every hope you have regarding your loved ones. Resolve to not give way to fear or doubt. Express your deepest desires to the Lord and write down each one. Then take time to pray through these hopes, dreams, and desires each day this week.

3. "Relieve the troubles of my heart and free me from my anguish." Ask the Lord to reveal to you any burdens, worries, or troubles that are causing you inner anguish. Make note of everything he reveals to you. Then enlist the support of a fellow believer, who will commit to pray alongside you to be full of faith, courage, and hope.

Truly my soul finds rest in God;
    my salvation comes from him.
Truly he is my rock and my salvation;
    he is my fortress, I will never be shaken. . . .

My salvation and my honor depend on God;
    he is my mighty rock, my refuge.
Trust in him at all times, you people;
    pour out your hearts to him,
    for God is our refuge. . . .

One thing God has spoken,
    two things I have heard:
"Power belongs to you, God,
    and with you, Lord, is unfailing love";
and, "You reward everyone
    according to what they have done."

PSALM 62

CHAPTER 21

Trusting God for Life after Death

Trusting God . . . means we work back through the Scriptures regarding His sovereignty, wisdom, and goodness and ask Him to use those Scriptures to bring peace and comfort to our hearts. It means, above all, that we do not sin against God by allowing distrustful and hard thoughts about Him to hold sway in our minds. It will often mean that we may have to say, "God I don't understand, but I trust You."

JERRY BRIDGES

J ay sat at the kitchen table flipping through the family's scrapbooks, sorting through photos he wanted to use for his sister's funeral—all the while doing his best to hold his emotions in check.

It was only three days ago that he had heard about the accident. It was one of those freak things where apparently no one was to blame. That dark early morning, the weather was foggy and wet when Jayne was driving home from work. None of the police officers or investigators knew exactly what had happened except that Jayne's SUV and another truck had somehow collided and rolled before both finally landed in the deep ditches bordering each side of the highway.

Jay picked up a photo and stared at it, remembering their family's recent holiday celebrations when he, Jayne, and their four siblings had spent both Christmas and New Year's Day together. It had been a rare feat indeed given how spread out the family was now that the "kids" had grown families of their own. As Jay looked through the photos, pausing on the ones of his sister, he just couldn't believe she was gone. It didn't seem real.

Paging through memory after memory, Jay's attention was riveted on one childhood scene in particular. Fingering the now-yellowed photo of himself, his siblings, and their parents, Jay sighed as he remembered when this picture was taken. It was right after their baptism at the lake. Five of the kids got dunked in the cold water and came up shivering. Dad and Mom had wrapped each of them in scratchy wool blankets, while they stood watching other church members be baptized. The only one who didn't get baptized was Jayne. She was so young, and their parents wanted her to be sure she understood what it meant to choose to follow Jesus. But that day never did come for Jayne, as far as anyone knew. When she was old enough to decide for herself about attending Sunday services or not, she opted out. Jay didn't recall if Jayne had ever shown a spark of interest in becoming a Christian.

Setting down the book, Jay let loose the emotion he'd been holding in. He recounted all the times through the years that he and the rest of the family had tried their best to woo Jayne back to church and to the Lord. They never preached at her. Instead, Jay and his family simply found ways to love Jayne and keep her close to the rest of them, despite their differences regarding faith. Now she was gone, and none of them could say with any assurance that Jayne ever made that decision to follow Christ.

All he knew was that his heart felt broken. He could only pray that God would help him find a way through this grief, to hold him up so he wouldn't give in to despair. For the truth is, no one but God alone knows the state of a human soul. Jay could only hope that before Jayne died she made her peace with her Creator and Lord.

"Power belongs to you, God,
    and with you, Lord, is unfailing love."

I'm sure many of us prayed even today for loved ones who have yet to make a commitment to Christ. Similarly, I'm sure there are moments when our faith wavers for them, our hope wanes, and we wonder if those we love will ever make the transition from spiritual death to eternal life. For my part, I've been praying for some family members for over forty-five years, and I've committed to the Lord to never cease praying until I see these dear folks make an about-face in their lives toward Jesus. But it isn't always easy.

Just as Jay chooses to cling to the hope that his sister Jayne may have made her own commitment to Jesus before she died, so must we choose that same faith-driven, peace-full, joy-full sentiment for those we love. Otherwise, our mingled grief and despair may render us ineffective and hopeless Christ followers. Truly, in the midst of our emotional sorrow, the only One who can provide the comfort we need at the deepest soul level is God himself. Only our loving heavenly Father is able to overcome our intellectual questioning, our mental puzzling, and our emotional despair. As in every difficult life scenario, especially in those life and death situations, the best and wisest choice is for us to pour our hearts out to God and wait for him to spread his ministering spirit over us, in us, and through us.

The truth is, there will be many occasions when it may appear as though God has not answered our prayers. It is in these extreme situations when we must shore up our confidence in God's sovereign power and unfailing love. In those heartrending life situations when all we feel is that rolling grief that comes upon us in waves, remember this: God promises to be our rock, our refuge, our fortress, and our mighty deliverer. There is no better response to a grieving soul than to pour out our deepest painful emotions to our loving heavenly Father.

Take-away Action Thought

When you feel undone by life-altering events with lasting ramifications, run to God and pour out your heart to him. Sit in a quiet place and meditate on the verses in Psalm 62, and wait on the Holy Spirit to bring the comfort you need to face this pain.

My Heart's Cry to You, O Lord

Father, without your enabling strength and grace, I don't think I could go on. I feel such grief and despair over the loss of my loved one that words cannot begin to describe my pain. If only I was sure that my dear one had made a commitment to you, I believe my grief would be manageable. But as it is, I am feeling nothing but deep soul sorrow. Oh, Lord, help me to keep my eyes on you. Remind me again and again that no one except for you knows the true state of a person's soul. Keep my hope alive and use this tender grief to motivate me to offer up better and more faithful service to you. Amen.

Deliver Us

1. "Truly my soul finds rest in God; my salvation comes from him." During those moments of severest emotional trauma, set yourself down before God and recount all the wondrous ways he has shown himself faithful to you through the years. Write down every act of faithfulness and revisit this list whenever you are tempted to doubt his wisdom and love for you.

2. "Trust in him at all times, you people; pour out your hearts to him, for God is our refuge." First thing in the morning and last thing in the evening, spend time alone with God sharing with him everything you're thinking and feeling. Keep an open dialogue going between you as you work through your grief. Make note of specific Bible promises that can help you journey through your sorrow.

3. "One thing God has spoken, two things I have heard: 'Power belongs to you, God, and with you, Lord, is unfailing love.'" As you continue to journey through this time of grief, spend time each day looking up verses that describe God's power and his unfailing love. Meditate on these twin principles to give you both perspective and hope as you grieve. Also pray that God helps you to grieve with a hopeful heart that fully trusts in him.

You are my God; have mercy on me, Lord,
    for I call to you all day long.
Bring joy to your servant, Lord,
    for I put my trust in you.

You, Lord, are forgiving and good,
    abounding in love to all who call to you.
Hear my prayer, Lord;
    listen to my cry for mercy.
When I am in distress, I call to you,
    because you answer me. . . .

Turn to me and have mercy on me;
    show your strength in behalf of your servant;
save me, because I serve you
    just as my mother did.
Give me a sign of your goodness,
    that my enemies may see it and be put to shame,
    for you, Lord, have helped me and comforted me.

PSALM 86

CHAPTER 22

Caring for Those Who
Don't Seem to Care

Realize God gives you strength one day at a time. He gives
you what you need when you need it. He doesn't encumber
you with excess baggage. God gives us His grace in the hour
we need it. If we worry about the future now, we double
our pain without having the grace to deal with it.

JOHN MACARTHUR

Meg looked down the street from the car dealership and then checked her phone—again. She typed out another text message but there was still no response. "Late as usual!" she said under her breath. This was rude. It was totally inconsiderate! Kelly knew Meg was trying to do this on her lunch hour. She would give her ten more minutes before she had to head back to the office. What was wrong with that girl? Didn't she realize what a big favor Meg was doing in helping her find a reliable car? Apparently not. Still fuming, Meg looked around the parking area to be sure she hadn't missed her. Not seeing her, Meg gave up and went inside the dealership to apologize profusely to the salesperson who had been helping Meg locate an affordable car for her baby sister.

As soon as she arrived back at work, Meg checked her phone again, but there was still no response. She tried to compose herself before she went inside to the PR firm where she worked as an advertising copywriter. She had no words, absolutely no words to express how angry she was. And for a copywriter, that was really saying something!

Once Meg put her phone on silent and started working on a new advertising campaign, though, she got lost in her work. The afternoon sped by more quickly than she had expected given how agitated she had been earlier. But Meg had learned one important lesson over the years of dealing with her younger, highly irresponsible sister—she had learned to move on. Since she knew she couldn't change her, she prayed for her on a regular basis and tried to be a godly example of sisterly love. She had learned a long time ago not to cross the line between caring and trying to strong-arm her sister into growing up.

Meg's act today of generosity in time and energy spent trying to help Kelly was now a rare occurrence, since Kelly had a habit of leaving her hanging like this. When Meg had first made these plans for meeting at the dealership, she figured the odds were 50/50 that Kelly would show up. Even though she knew this and even expected it, she was still angry at her inconsiderate sister. Meg longed for her to take responsibility for her actions. After all, at twenty-eight, Kelly was an adult. So why did she still behave as though she were thirteen?

Meg took a deep breath and prayed for wisdom and restraint as she tried to love and serve her sister. She knew that there was nothing she could say or do that would change her. But she knew that God could do a wonderful work within her heart and mind. In the meantime, she could only ask for God's help to love her unconditionally—while not being afraid to set up healthy boundaries so that Kelly didn't dismantle Meg's life as she often did her own. For now, she would forgive Kelly as God forgave her. Meg knew that she herself was far from perfect, so she prayed for the grace she needed to deal with her sister.

> You, Lord, are forgiving and good,
>   abounding in love to all who call to you.
> Hear my prayer, LORD;
>   listen to my cry for mercy.
> When I am in distress, I call to you,
>   because you answer me.

Meg is one among many responsible sisters and brothers, mothers and fathers, friends and neighbors, who love their irresponsible family members dearly but have learned the same important lesson: boundaries are essential. It is the right choice to love your dear one. It is another thing altogether to allow their irresponsible lifestyle to pull apart your own. So, good boundaries must be set in place and then heeded.

Certainly, our loving heavenly Father never wants us to give up on those he has placed in our lives. The encouraging truth is that there is always hope for lasting change in the heart and mind of every one of us. The challenge, however, comes when we discover that loving our irresponsible family members or friends can cost us dearly. Their inaction or poor decisions may affect us (as much or more) than it affects them.

Since Kelly chose not to show up as promised, Meg's efforts were wasted. And let's not minimize how much emotional and mental energy Meg expended each time Kelly pulled another irresponsible stunt. It is expensive, emotionally speaking, to continue investing in a person who repeatedly undoes your good work on their behalf.

Like Meg, whenever any of us find ourselves embroiled in a relationship with someone from whom we cannot extricate ourselves, we must decide on healthy boundaries. If we are to go the long haul with that person, then we must hold fast to the good Lord's hand and lean on him for daily (sometimes hourly!) strength to endure the uncomfortable, the unlovable, even the incomprehensible behavior from them. We hold on to hope for their sake by taking our direction from the Lord, likewise holding them to the high standard of conduct he expects of us for our good and his glory.

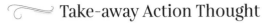 Take-away Action Thought

When you feel like giving up on your loved one because their irresponsibility has caused you personal pain and frustration, retreat to a quiet place and ask the Lord to give you his perfect, eternal perspective on the situation. Don't give up on them, but hold them accountable for their choices because, over the long run, you want what is best for them.

My Heart's Cry to You, O Lord

Father, my loved one disappointed me again, and I'm irritated and upset. I tried to calm down by telling myself I shouldn't expect more of this person, but I do. I want to believe they can and will change. I see so much potential in them, more than they see in themselves. Help me to not get sidetracked by my recent disappointment and frustration. Help me to lean on you for the grace I need to keep loving them within the framework of healthy boundaries. Give me the wisdom to know how to speak truth into their life. Please open their heart and mind to hear it. I rely fully on you to do something magnificent in my loved one's life. Amen.

Deliver Us

1. "Bring joy to your servant, Lord, for I put my trust in you." When you are mired in the emotional stress of trying to love your dear but careless one, spend time (both in quality and quantity) renewing your mind daily by reading the Bible, praying, listening to praise music, reading helpful books, and listening to sermons. Make it a priority to invest in feeding your soul.

2. "Turn to me and have mercy on me; show your strength on behalf of your servant; save me." Each time you feel worn out by your loved one's irresponsible choices, don't allow their poor decisions

to dismantle your life. Instead, close your eyes, be still, and remember that God promises to provide strength for everything you need to navigate difficult relationships responsibly.

3. "Give me a sign of your goodness, that my enemies may see it and be put to shame." In those moments when you want to give up on your dear one, pray all the more diligently. Write down in your journal every positive decision or action that you have observed them make so you can find some praiseworthy choices on which you can focus.

How good and pleasant it is
    when God's people live together in unity!

It is like precious oil poured on the head,
    running down on the beard,
running down on Aaron's beard,
    down on the collar of his robe.
It is as if the dew of Hermon
    were falling on Mount Zion.
For there the LORD bestows his blessing,
    even life forevermore.

PSALM 133

CHAPTER 23

Prevailing Love, Regardless

*In all your suffering, He suffers. He is with you, right in the midst
of it. Helping you. Loving you. Hurting with you. Driving you
back to Him, drawing you closer in, making you more dependent
upon His grace and power. As you get to know and trust His
heart, you will be able to face the cross—the way Christ faced
it from the haunting shadows of Gethsemane—and still say,
even through your tears, "Not my will, but Yours be done."*

NANCY LEIGH DEMOSS

They *what!*" I couldn't believe that I had heard correctly. "Why did they change their minds? Don't they realize you sold your house and already moved into the new place? This doesn't make any sense!"

Jenna, my lifelong and dearest friend, then reiterated to me what I viewed as inexplicable and unreal. Her parents had just told her that they had changed their minds about sharing a home with her and her three children, that they decided they wanted to stay in their own home. She then told me she was heading over to her parents' house to try and talk some sense into them. "After all," she said, "moving in together was their idea, not mine! They even picked out the house they wanted. What am I supposed to do now? There is no way I can afford this new house on my income. I can't believe my parents did this to us. I uprooted the kids and everything for them!"

Jenna had a right to be angry and frustrated by this sudden decision. When her parents had first suggested sharing a house, she had tried to squelch this idea. She had been reluctant to say yes, knowing how difficult and unbending both of her parents were. Over time and with a lot of prayer, however, she agreed to combine households when she realized she would eventually end up being her parents' primary caregiver anyway.

It took a while for Jenna to understand what was behind this sudden decision not to follow through with their plan, but she finally realized that it was simply that her parents hated any type of change. Perhaps the saddest part of this story is that Jenna's parents didn't believe they had done anything wrong. They took no responsibility for their actions, which cost their daughter more money than she could afford. As a result, she was forced to sell the new house at a loss, and she and her three children moved into an apartment until she was able to afford another home some years later.

Understandably, Jenna's emotions did flip-flops and backflips for a long time. She had to work through painful memories, present injuries, and the possibility of future injustices from her parents. Over time, she did come full circle and forgave them even though they never so much as offered an apology. She then made peace with the fact that her parents would probably never treat her with the love and respect she desired from them. Instead, she purposed to love her parents one day at a time, through the supernatural empowering of the Holy Spirit. Everyone who knew her—and her parents—marveled at how, despite everything that had happened, love prevailed. Even though she wouldn't physically be living with her parents, she could focus on at least getting along with them, regardless.

> How good and pleasant it is
>   when God's people live together in unity!

Although this story happened many years ago, the stinging scenario continues to live on vividly in my memory. I was in awe of my dear friend's ability to love, serve, and relate peaceably to her parents after their disastrous turnabout decision. Despite the cost to my friend and her children, Jenna leaned hard on the Lord's strength and grace to go beyond forgiveness. She blessed her parents, and she made sure her mother and father had everything they needed until the end of their days. Jenna visited several times a week at their old home, and she called at least once a day to check in with them. She still acted as their primary caregiver: she took them to every appointment they had, she shopped for them, she helped clean their home, and she cooked as needed. Jenna truly exhibited a prevailing love for her parents for Jesus' sake.

Although very few of us will ever be placed into a similar situation as extreme as Jenna's, we will still have times when we need to decide if we will obey God and forgive those who sin against us, and then go a step farther and choose to bless our offender. Let's be honest. The struggle is real. But Jenna told me how she managed to continue serving, loving, and pursuing a unified, peaceable relationship with her parents. She knew that whatever she suffered Jesus suffered right along with her. She knew that Jesus was working in her to drive her nearer to his perfect love; and in the process, he was remaking Jenna into his own image. Jenna also told me, "Just knowing that Jesus sits at the right hand of the Father interceding on my behalf—well, it makes my small measure of suffering endurable."

May we all follow Jenna's eternity-focused example. May we learn to quickly forgive. May we learn to bless our offenders. May we learn to pray, "Not my will, but your will be done." As Paul reminds us, "But God demonstrates his own love for us in this: While we were still sinners, Christ died for us" (Rom. 5:8). Prevailing love, regardless. It is indeed possible.

⌒ Take-away Action Thought

When you feel the stinging pain of someone's offense against you, choose to obey God's command to forgive quickly. Then pray and ask the Lord for the strength and grace to go a step farther than forgiveness by asking God to help you bless your offender so that his perfect love can prevail.

My Heart's Cry to You, O Lord

Father, I could not have imagined a more painful scenario than the one I am facing. And to think that those closest to me are the ones who have brought this pain into my life. It's almost too much to bear. Please, Lord, help me to forgive them. Give me the grace I need to go a step farther and even bless them. I know that in my own strength, I will fail. It is my heart's desire to honor you by trusting you to transform this disastrous situation into something good. I know that you suffer with me and that you are going to do a deeper work in my heart and mind than I can conceive. Lord, come close to me and help me to have the courage to pray, "Not my will, but your will be done." Amen.

Deliver Us

1. "How good and pleasant it is when God's people live together in unity!" Each morning this week, commit your difficult situation into the Lord's keeping. Cast off the burdens and worries you have been holding on to and pray for the Lord to give you the grace you need to live as peaceably as possible with those who have sinned against you.

2. "It is like precious oil poured on the head." This week, do a word search and read biblical accounts of those stories where the words *precious oil* are included, so as to more fully understand this type of analogy as it pertains to prevailing love that seeks unity in relationships.

3. "The Lord bestows his blessing, even life forevermore." Each evening this week, be mindful and thankful for all the goodness God has brought into your life. Make note of each of God's blessings to you to remind yourself that even in the midst of this difficult situation, there is so much good for which to give thanks.

How lovely is your dwelling place,
    Lord Almighty!
My soul yearns, even faints,
    for the courts of the Lord;
my heart and my flesh cry out
    for the living God.
Even the sparrow has found a home,
    and the swallow a nest for herself,
    where she may have her young—
a place near your altar,
    Lord Almighty, my King and my God.
Blessed are those who dwell in your house;
    they are ever praising you.

Blessed are those whose strength is in you,
    whose hearts are set on pilgrimage. . . .
They go from strength to strength,
    till each appears before God in Zion. . . .

For the Lord God is a sun and shield;
    the Lord bestows favor and honor;
no good thing does he withhold
    from those whose walk is blameless.

            Psalm 84

CHAPTER 24

Sheltering and Loving a Needy Grandchild

Your hope of enduring is not to be found in your character or strength, but in your Lord's. Because he will ever be faithful, you can bank on the fact that he will give you what you need to be faithful too. Your perseverance rests on him, and he defines what endurance looks like! When difficulty exposes the weakness of your resolve and the limits of your strength, you do not have to panic, because he will endure even in those moments when you don't feel able to do so yourself.

Paul David Tripp

A llie had been a single mom and now, in her late sixties, she is a single grandmother. After her daughter, Leann, died of an overdose two years earlier, Allie was awarded full custody of her seven-year-old granddaughter, Emme. On most days, Allie is exhausted by the time her head hits the pillow at night; and on those particularly trying days, she honestly wonders if she has what it takes to parent her Emme to adulthood. The irony is that it's not little Emme who depletes Allie's energy levels; it's Emme's biological father's side of the family, who had done nothing to help this child after she lost her mother, and her father disappeared from her life. What really wearies Allie is her fruitless effort to get these other adults to love Emme and put her welfare above their own.

One night not too long ago, Allie told me how she and Emme were all ready for bed and settling down to read a few books before bedtime when the phone rang. When she saw that it was Grandma

Helen calling, she almost didn't answer it. It was a school night and it was already getting late, but maybe it was an emergency. Grandma Helen did have a heart condition. It turned out Allie was right about that heart condition, though it had nothing to do with any medical problems.

Helen abruptly told her that she was on her way over there. As Allie started getting dressed again, she saw the joy on Emme's face when she told her that Grandma Helen was coming over. Although she had regretted answering the phone and allowing this woman to come over so late on a school night, she was now hopeful that it would be a pleasant visit—something that Emme desperately needed from her other grandmother and that side of the family.

Some fifty minutes later, and now well past Emme's bedtime, car lights finally flashed in the driveway. When Emme saw Grandma Helen in the doorway, she jumped up and ran forward with open arms. But instead of leaning down to hug her grandchild, Helen brushed past her to a chair, throwing her purse and coat onto it. Then she launched into an unexpected tirade. "I can't stay here any longer! There's nothing for me in this town. Nothing! I'm leaving first thing in the morning for Texas, and I'm not coming back—ever!"

Allie inhaled sharply and looked over at little Emme, hoping she didn't understand the implications of what Grandma Helen was saying. Allie wished she'd heeded her first instinct to not answer the phone. What was Emme supposed to think of the fact that her other grandmother just said there was nothing for her here? What about her darling granddaughter? Emme had already lost both of her parents, and this little girl needed what remained of her family. How could this woman be so selfish? How could she not see what a blessing Emme was?

For an hour, Helen ranted about her pitiful life and how everyone took advantage of her—and it was all Allie could do to control her own temper and her tongue. Finally, just before leaving, Helen looked at Emme and said, "You've grown up, Emme. I'll bet Grandma Allie has a hard time affording all the clothes you grow out of."

Emme just stared at Grandma Helen, silent.

Allie smiled at the child and quickly said, "Emme *is* growing up, and she is doing so well in school. Emme was even selected to represent her class in the spelling contest next month. Isn't that something? Emme's a smart, bright girl. I'm so proud of her!"

"Uh-huh," Helen said disinterestedly. "Well, I'm off. Goodbye, Allie. Goodbye, Emme. Be good for your grandma." And that was that.

Allie had never been so glad to shut the door on someone than she was at that moment. That was enough! That woman had done all the harm she was ever going to do to Emme. She hugged the girl and then tucked her back into bed. As she smoothed the hair from her little face, she beseeched God to help her protect her granddaughter from those heartless people who didn't know what real love looked like.

> Even the sparrow has found a home,
>   and the swallow a nest for herself,
>   where she may have her young—
> a place near your altar.

Folks like Allie are my real-life heroes, because they take on real-time responsibilities that are beyond their human capabilities. At Allie's age, and given her many health issues, she is that rare faith-full woman who says yes when it would have been so much easier to say no. For the sake of her granddaughter, Allie dedicates the very best she has to give so that Emme can grow up in a loving, faith-driven, stable home. God bless her efforts. And God does.

Allie would be the first to say that parenting a second time around does not get any easier. In fact, in many ways it is more difficult because of age, limited energy, and the challenges of dealing with children. And still, Allie knows from whom she will get the grace and stamina she needs to face each day. This self-sacrificing woman wisely invests her early morning hours to communing with God, delving deeply into his word, and writing out at least one Scripture verse to carry with her through the day. When she begins to feel overwhelmed by any number of challenges, she then pulls out that precious promise and reads it aloud to herself.

Allie will tell anyone who will listen that when God asks you to serve in a way you may consider difficult, he will provide whatever you need to fulfill that task. She knows this from personal experience!

> Blessed are those whose strength is in you,
> whose hearts are set on pilgrimage. . . .
> They go from strength to strength,
> till each appears before God in Zion.

As he is doing with Allie, surely God will strengthen us also one day, one act of service at a time.

◠◡ Take-away Action Thought

When you become overwhelmed by circumstances beyond your control and don't feel you have the strength to continue, stop, pray, and recite those Bible verses (especially the Psalms) that speak of God's promises to provide you with strength and grace for your every need.

My Heart's Cry to You, O Lord

Father, today I encountered another troubling family situation that I am powerless to correct. There is nothing I can do in my own strength to bring healing and wholeness to this family. I have tried to open my heart and my home to these troubled souls, but now I must become firm with protective boundaries. Help me to be wise and yet always compassionate. Help me to know what is best for those under my care. Please, Lord, I am feeling depleted and discouraged. I need to focus solely on your unchanging love and your promise to give me the strength I require day by day. My hope is found only in you, Lord. Amen.

Deliver Us

1. "My soul yearns, even faints, for the courts of the Lord; my heart and my flesh cry out for the living God." This week, do a word search for verses that include *living God*, and then take the time to look them up and read them. Meditate on the profound truth and impact that the living God has on you and upon your life.

2. "Blessed are those whose strength is in you, whose hearts are set on pilgrimage. . . . They go from strength to strength." Read a classic Christian book, such as *The Pilgrim's Progress* by John Bunyan, to remind you that you too are a pilgrim in this land and on your way to somewhere better.

3. "For the Lord God is a sun and shield; the Lord bestows favor and honor; no good thing does he withhold from those whose walk is blameless." This week, list all the occasions you can recall when the Lord gave you "good things" whether in the form of words of encouragement, Bible promises, worship songs, beauty found in the natural world, or even material things. Review this list as a reminder of how God loves you in a personal and generous way—every day.

How long, LORD? Will you forget me forever?
    How long will you hide your face from me?
How long must I wrestle with my thoughts
    and day after day have sorrow in my heart?
    How long will my enemy triumph over me?

Look on me and answer, LORD my God.
    Give light to my eyes, or I will sleep in death,
and my enemy will say, "I have overcome him,"
    and my foes will rejoice when I fall.

But I trust in your unfailing love;
    my heart rejoices in your salvation.
I will sing the LORD's praise,
    for he has been good to me.

PSALM 13

CHAPTER 25

Staying Sturdy on Rocky Ground

*Sometimes we will perceive quite clearly what God is doing,
and in those instances we should respond to God's teaching in
humble obedience. At other times, we may not be able to see
at all what He is doing in our lives. At those times, we should
respond in humble faith, trusting Him to work out in our lives
that which we need to learn. Both attitudes are important, and
God wants one at one time and the other at another time.*

JERRY BRIDGES

For as long as Randy could remember, he had dreamed of taking over his family's farming operation. It had been run by his grandfather and then by his father, and Randy believed that this life and legacy was bred into his DNA. It was where he had been born and raised. As he grew up, he arose before the sun and worked alongside his father until it was time to leave for school. But he felt confined in the classroom and couldn't wait to get back out into the fields where he felt at home. Despite his reluctance, he did well in school. In fact, everything came easy to him—schoolwork, sports, and trying his hand at increasingly difficult farming tasks.

In high school, Randy earned scholarships because of his excellent GPA and athletic abilities. At the insistence of his parents, he attended the nearby college and earned his bachelor of science degree. His parents wanted their son to have options in life. After years of running their farm, they saw the tides of change coming. While they earnestly hoped to keep the farm in operation into future generations, no one could anticipate how ever-altering markets could affect it. Still,

Randy persisted in working toward his dream of taking over the farm when his father stepped back from the job.

Fast-forward fifteen years: post-college graduation and married with three children, Randy was happily living out his dream. He had learned to weather the unpredictable seasons of drought or the opposite, as too much rain greatly reduced the crops that could be harvested. If anyone could endure the changing weather patterns, the constant revisions in the law, and ever-increasing prices for equipment, maintenance, and seed supplies, it was Randy.

But when a trifecta of unexpected events occurred, even Randy couldn't make the impossible work. First, his wife endured a difficult delivery of their third child, which resulted in expensive medical bills and treatments. Then a series of machinery breakdowns required purchasing new combines. Finally, the record-breaking rainfall from early spring through midsummer prevented him from planting two-thirds of his land.

Randy met often with his banker, who tried to extend loans, refinance his mortgage, and come up with other cost-saving solutions—but to no avail. In shock and disbelief, Randy realized he was on the cusp of losing everything for which he had worked his entire life, and he had run out of ideas for how to fix the situation.

Although he may not have had the answers to his questions, he knew where to turn for help and guidance. Randy purposed in his heart to trust God and be obedient in whatever God led him to do next. He knew he was in good hands.

> But I trust in your unfailing love;
> my heart rejoices in your salvation.
> I will sing the LORD's praise,
> for he has been good to me.

At the time of this writing, many people within our circle of acquaintances are facing similar frightening scenarios like Randy.

Small businesses are closing their doors. Job layoffs are increasing daily with little hope for rehiring. Dreams small and large are evaporating all around us. Those closest to us have shared how shocked they feel by the radical suddenness of such life-altering events. And they are not alone.

Like Randy, there are countless examples of hardworking men and women who went to their place of employment, eager to apply their talents to the task at hand, only to be told that their job had been eliminated. How then can any of us survive these unexpected tsunami waves that are wreaking havoc all around us?

Of course, we look to God for the answers to these seemingly insurmountable problems. First, we turn to God in humble obedience, continuing to behave in a way that brings honor and glory to our heavenly Father. We continue to react in a way fitting for a child of God. Our attitude is to keep doing the right thing, making choices that fall in line with what God's word tells us. Second, we turn to God in humble faith, trusting him to do in our lives (and in us) what he deems best for our ultimate good and his glory. We align our hearts with the biblical truth that God oversees the entirety of our lives, orchestrating even the minutest details behind the scenes.

Only when we put into daily practice these two principles of faith—obedience and trust—can we take a deep breath and exhale all our fears and broken dreams. When we release our grip on our dearest hope, our most precious dream, only then can we experience the blessed freedom of acceptance that God wants from us. But, oh, when we do "give back" to God what we treasure, then he begins what he does best: a work of transformation in divine proportions! Our part is to trust and obey. God's part is to do the impossible by redeeming even that which we believed was lost forever.

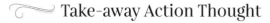
Take-away Action Thought

When you begin to lose faith that your dream will ever become a reality or that your life will return to "normal," remember to put your trust in God and obey however he leads you. Turn to the Lord in faith and then do the "next thing," one day a time.

My Heart's Cry to You, O Lord

Father, help me to remember that though I'm grieving this huge loss in my life right now, I can live one day at a time, trusting in your perfect plan for me. In truth, I do feel grief-stricken by this unexpected avalanche that has left me feeling buried. I never saw this life-altering event coming. Please help me to surrender the desires of my heart to you. Give me the grace I need to endure this season of frightening transition and hopeful new beginnings. Above all, help me to behave as one of your beloved children by humbly trusting you and obeying you. Amen.

Deliver Us

1. "How long must I wrestle with my thoughts and day after day have sorrow in my heart?" Before you go to sleep, spend time alone with the Lord telling him all about your day. Share with him your joys, sorrows, and yet-unfulfilled dreams. Then sing a song of praise as a way of demonstrating your trust in your loving Savior, no matter what is happening in your life.

2. "But I trust in your unfailing love; my heart rejoices in your salvation." Each morning this week, spend time in the Psalms reading through the verses that speak of praising and rejoicing in your salvation. Remind yourself that "his divine power has given us everything we need for a godly life through our knowledge of him

who called us by his own glory and goodness" (2 Pet. 1:3). Dwell on the amazing permanence of this blessed truth.

3. "I will sing the LORD's praise, for he has been good to me." Every day this week, be purposeful about playing (and singing) praise and worship music at home, in your car, in your office, anytime and anywhere you can. Saturate your heart and mind with theological truths that will help you put into proper perspective the personal trials you are experiencing.

Praise the LORD, my soul,
    and forget not all his benefits—
who forgives all your sins
    and heals all your diseases. . . .

As a father has compassion on his children,
    so the LORD has compassion on those who fear him;
for he knows how we are formed,
    he remembers that we are dust.
The life of mortals is like grass,
    they flourish like a flower of the field;
the wind blows over it and it is gone,
    and its place remembers it no more.
But from everlasting to everlasting
    the LORD's love is with those who fear him,
        and his righteousness with their children's children.

PSALM 103

CHAPTER 26

Loving Those Who Seem Unlovable

We may think we have true Christian love until someone offends us or treats us unjustly. Then we begin to see anger and resentment well up within us. We may conclude we have learned about genuine Christian joy until our lives are shattered by an unexpected calamity or grievous disappointment. Adversities spoil our peace and sorely try our patience. God uses those difficulties to reveal to us our need to grow, so that we will reach out to Him to change us more and more into the likeness of His Son. He will not remove the adversity until we have profited from it and developed in whatever way He intended in bringing or allowing it into our lives.

JERRY BRIDGES

C hristie and Greg had been married for over thirty years—thirty long and difficult years, she often thought. If it hadn't been for the grace of God, she would have given up long ago and divorced Greg. From the very beginning, his talk didn't match his walk. He said he was a Christian. He said he loved Christie. He said he wanted to be a good father to their two children. He said he would get a steady job. He said he would quit drinking. And Christie's response to all that was to say, "If I had a dollar for every one of Greg's empty promises, I would be a rich woman today!"

Although she hated to admit it, Christie was becoming angrier with Greg every day, and her patience had run about as low as his last bottle of whiskey. Sometimes late at night, that anger melted into a feeling of despair, into a hopelessness that he would ever change. In the morning when she got up, she often spent the first ninety minutes sequestered alone in her home office. Knowing Greg wouldn't be up for a while yet, she could read her Bible, pray, and write in her journal. Once in a while, she took the time to sit with a helpful devotional.

While Christie worked hard to buoy herself up in the word of God and through prayer, it was the ongoing feelings of loneliness that she battled hardest against. Sure, she was married. But unless Greg's life changed in a dramatic way, Christie felt herself manacled to this unbelieving, unloving, and supremely selfish man. But even though this assessment of her husband was accurate, she realized that she wasn't entirely blameless. She began to understand that she had been expecting too much of him over the years, and that she had also become selfish by wanting to be treated well by him when he couldn't manage to treat himself any better. Although Greg's attitude and actions were light-years away from how she imagined a godly husband should be, Christie slowly began to recognize that she had hardened her heart against him over the course of their marriage.

Now that Christie has realized that she's been part of the problem in this relationship, she is taking a different tack. Instead of nursing unrealistic expectations of Greg that only serve to spark fresh resentment and ongoing disappointment, Christie prays for God's grace to live peaceably, contentedly, and joyfully. She continues to pray diligently for her husband, and she also holds him accountable for his choices. But she no longer expects him to give her everything she needs and desires. This is an impossible task for even the most considerate of men! Instead, Christie has finally learned that only God can provide her heart's desire and meet her every need.

> Praise the LORD, my soul;
>   all my inmost being, praise his holy name.
> Praise the LORD, my soul,
>   and forget not all his benefits.

How I wish we could all jump in at the place in Christie's story where she realizes that her best and brightest source of love, acceptance, hope, and help will always come from the Lord. But in real life, aren't we all a lot like Christie? We spend weeks, months—years even— trying to manipulate people to better suit us. Of course, we do it in the name of thinking we know what's best for everyone concerned, ourselves included. But truthfully, how much effort do we waste trying to change what only God can change? We believe our motives are pure when we tell those hard-to-love individuals in our lives that they need to make an about-face in their attitude and actions or else.

Like Christie, I admit to focusing too much on how I think people should treat me, when I should be far more mindful of how I treat others. Those who seem the most unlovable are usually the very ones who need the most love.

I've often told my children that it is much wiser to learn a difficult lesson the first time around. Otherwise, you'll just have to keep riding that same bus around until you do. And often, God's ways of grabbing our attention get bigger, louder, and more painful with each trip. Jerry Bridges hit me squarely in the heart when I read his words,

> God uses those difficulties to reveal to us our need to grow, so that we will reach out to Him to change us more and more into the likeness of His Son. He will not remove the adversity until we have profited from it and developed in whatever way He intended in bringing or allowing it into our lives.

From today forward, therefore, let us purpose to love the seemingly unlovable with God's grace and strength. Let us discard our false idols of unrealistic expectations at his feet. And let us willingly embrace the difficulties God allows in our lives as agents of change that will conform us more closely into the image of his Son, our Savior, Jesus.

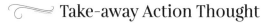 Take-away Action Thought

When you start to feel anger and resentment build up inside, quickly rebuke those unhealthy, ungodly thoughts and say aloud instead something uplifting and positive about your situation. Do not allow yourself to become mired in negativity or despair.

My Heart's Cry to You, O Lord

Father, today is a brand-new day. It's a fresh start. Please help me to keep my heart and my mind focused on you alone. Help me to cast away any idols that have become stumbling blocks in my relationships with others. I know that only you are capable of meeting my every need. And yet, I sometimes wrongly place unrealistic burdens on those nearest and dearest to me. This doesn't do any of us any good. Help me to look to you alone to sustain me in this life. And give me the grace I need to overcome evil with good, by loving those whom I deem most unlovable. Amen.

Deliver Us

1. "Praise the LORD, my soul, and forget not all his benefits." Each morning this week, before you begin interacting with others, spend time alone with God in Bible reading and prayer. Keep these daily appointments with God, understanding that you need to remember all the good he has done for you and how he will help you overcome your current difficulties.

2. "Who crowns you with love and compassion, who satisfies your desires with good things." Each day this week, remind yourself of specific events when you witnessed God's faithfulness toward you. Write down these events so you can refer to them whenever you feel overwhelmed by the challenges in your life. Be a good remember-er!

3. "As a father has compassion on his children, so the LORD has compassion on those who fear him; for he knows how we are formed, he remembers that we are dust." This week, intentionally make contact with the difficult people in your life and ask each one how they are doing. Listen to them as they share their struggles and then commit to pray for them. The following week, call again and follow up with them so they know you are committed to loving them, despite your relational challenges.

Ascribe to the LORD, you heavenly beings,
　　ascribe to the LORD glory and strength.
Ascribe to the LORD the glory due his name;
　　worship the LORD in the splendor of his holiness.

The voice of the LORD is over the waters;
　　the God of glory thunders,
　　the LORD thunders over the mighty waters.
The voice of the LORD is powerful;
　　the voice of the LORD is majestic. . . .

The voice of the LORD strikes
　　with flashes of lightning. . . .
The voice of the LORD twists the oaks
　　and strips the forests bare.
And in his temple all cry, "Glory!"

The LORD sits enthroned over the flood;
　　the LORD is enthroned as King forever.
The LORD gives strength to his people;
　　the LORD blesses his people with peace.

PSALM 29

CHAPTER 27

Mourning That Leads to Happy Anticipation

It is when your soul has been blasted bare, when you feel raw and undone, that you can be better bonded to the Savior. And then you not only meet suffering on God's terms, but you meet joy on God's terms. And then God . . . happily shares his gladness, his joy flooding over heaven's walls filling my heart in a waterfall of delight, which then in turn always streams out to others in a flood of encouragement, and then erupts back to God in an ecstatic fountain of praise. He gets your heart pumping for heaven.

JONI EARECKSON TADA

I have nine grandchildren. Five of my grands are the absolute joy of my life. The remaining four I've yet to meet. This is because my oldest daughter, Nicole, and my middle daughter, Katlyn, suffered two heartbreaking miscarriages each.

I remember when my daughters and their husbands were excited and delighted to tell us when they became pregnant. I still recall those tender, celebratory moments and hold them deep within my mother's heart. Sadly, I also remember the phone calls from my girls asking us to pray, because they feared they were losing their babies. Each time, they were right.

Although the circumstances and the surrounding medical issues were unique to their pregnancies and subsequent miscarriages, the grief suffered was the same. As a mom who watched them endure not only the physical trauma of delivering their unborn babies but also the hard process of mourning, I felt helpless as I grieved alongside them. It was a difficult season for all of us as we trusted the Lord and his perfect plan for us, while being blindsided by shock and pain at the same time.

Our faith made all the difference. Yes, we all suffered. Yes, we all mourned. Yes, we endured grief and some measure of depression. But we never experienced hopelessness, because we know our Redeemer lives. And because our lives are eternally secure through Jesus' sacrifice on the cross, we believe we will have all of eternity to get to know and love these four precious ones who went ahead of us to be in the presence of the Lord. I'm reminded of the words from that old hymn,

> My hope is built on nothing less
> Than Jesus' blood and righteousness.
> I dare not trust the sweetest frame,
> But wholly lean on Jesus' name.
> On Christ the solid rock I stand,
> All other ground is sinking sand,
> All other ground is sinking sand.

As we worked through our sorrow, we also learned to sing with a new song in our hearts—a song that joyfully proclaims the everlasting goodness of God, no matter how grim our circumstances. Sound incredible? Not when you are one of God's beloved children and you know his love, his goodness, and his grand plan that will span all of eternity.

> Ascribe to the LORD, you heavenly beings,
>   ascribe to the LORD glory and strength.
> Ascribe to the LORD the glory due his name;
>   worship the LORD in the splendor of his holiness.

One of the rather unexpected and amazing lessons that I gleaned during those seasons of grief and loss was this: mourning eventually is transformed into a happy anticipation. It's true. When we are in the midst of sorrow, our emotions can pulsate with seemingly unbearable intensity or flatline into numbness. Either way, when the shock begins to wear off after a while, we then have to decide which way we will go. Will we allow our suffering and loss to lead us to resisting God or even walking away (or *trying* to walk away) from him? Or will we surrender our wills to his sovereign plan and trust him even when we do not understand?

As my family and I moved past our grief, I began to take note of the remarkable statements my daughters made when they referred to their respective losses. They both started to talk of being intentional about praising the Lord for his strength, grace, and goodness during their darkest, bleakest moments. They detailed specific blessings and the "good" things that came into their lives at just the right moment, which they both attributed to God's tender care. For my part, I purposefully disciplined myself to begin my day with thanksgiving and praise, every day without fail. And before long, as is always true in God's economy, when I honored him with my trust and thanked him by faith for what I anticipated he was going to do through these heartaches, I felt my joy explode much as Joni Tada related in the quotation above.

My sorrow was transformed into a heavenly and happy anticipation of what I can look forward to in the great tomorrow. My heartache softened me to become a more caring, sensitive, and compassionate woman. My faith didn't shield me from the pain of losing those four grandchildren, but it did get my "heart pumping for heaven"!

⌒ Take-away Action Thought

When you feel overwhelmed by sorrow, begin praising the Lord for his goodness, faithfulness, and enduring love. Read through the book of Psalms and speak out loud those passages that get your "heart pumping for heaven."

My Heart's Cry to You, O Lord

Father, this morning when I awoke, I briefly forgot about my grief. Then I remembered, and my heart immediately plummeted again. I want to wake up every morning looking for the new mercies you have promised us as your beloved children. But sometimes, my heart feels like it is going to fail me. I'm so very sad. Help me to turn to your promises and remember the wonderful truth of eternal life. Give me a fresh and so-needed eternal perspective that will temper my suffering. Show me how to grieve and then find encouragement and fresh joy, because you are near me and will never forsake me. I want to go deeper in my faith and in my knowledge of who you are. Please give me the wisdom I need today to accept your divine and perfect will for my life. Amen.

Deliver Us

1. "Ascribe to the LORD, you heavenly beings, ascribe to the LORD glory and strength." This week, instead of giving way to unending sorrow, play praise music in your home, car, at your desk, wherever and whenever you are able. At the close of each day, take a few moments to reflect on the Lord's glory and strength, knowing that these two proactive spiritual disciplines will jumpstart the healing within your heart.

2. "The voice of the LORD is powerful; the voice of the LORD is majestic." Conduct a word search through the Bible, looking up verses that speak of the Lord's power and majesty. Then jot down any accompanying thoughts you have that bring you confidence in God's perfect plan for you.

3. "The LORD gives strength to his people; the LORD blesses his people with peace." Each morning this week, locate a new verse that speaks of the Lord blessing his people with peace. Select one verse each day and write it down to carry with you, so you can refer to its wonderful promise as often as you have need.

I will extol the LORD at all times;
    his praise will always be on my lips.
I will glory in the LORD;
    let the afflicted hear and rejoice.
Glorify the LORD with me;
    let us exalt his name together.

I sought the LORD, and he answered me;
    he delivered me from all my fears.
Those who look to him are radiant;
    their faces are never covered with shame.
This poor man called, and the LORD heard him;
    he saved him out of all his troubles. . . .

Taste and see that the LORD is good;
    blessed is the one who takes refuge in him.
Fear the LORD, you his holy people,
    for those who fear him lack nothing. . . .

The righteous cry out, and the LORD hears them;
    he delivers them from all their troubles.
The LORD is close to the brokenhearted
    and saves those who are crushed in spirit.

The righteous person may have many troubles,
    but the LORD delivers him from them all.

PSALM 34

CHAPTER 28

Praising Instead of Complaining

*As white is to black, so is contentment to complaints and
anxiety. The Christian's Excalibur against the dragon
Anxiety is named Contentment. It likewise is the banner
under which Christ's troops advance to personal victory.*

JOHN MACARTHUR

Marsha sat perched on her chair with purse, phone, and keys in hand as she waited for the driver to arrive. Taking a quick glance at the time, she started getting anxious when she realized the car should have been there ten minutes ago. If she was late, her appointment would be canceled and she'd have to reschedule. She'd already been waiting eight weeks to see this specialist. Looking up, she exhaled in relief as she saw a white SUV pull into her driveway.

"I'm glad you're here!" Marsha said as she slid into the backseat. "I was afraid I might miss my doctor's appointment. But I think I'll make it." Putting on her seatbelt, Marsha looked at her driver. Wanting to be friendly, she introduced herself and asked the driver how long she had been working for this company.

The driver introduced herself as Dee and then responded, "I've been driving for them for about six months now. I'm a single mom, and I'm going to school at the college in town. I try to pick up as many rides as I can, in between driving my son to school and going to my college classes. I like it though. I've met so many interesting people."

"I worked at that college until last year—until my stroke, that is," Marsha shared. "After I got out of the hospital, I spent months trying to regain my strength, but some of my cognitive abilities haven't returned."

"I'm sorry to hear that. If you don't mind me asking—because you look terrific—what exactly can't you do that you used to?"

"Well, for starters, I can't read and I was an English professor. For me, reading is like breathing. The funny thing is, I can write words out fine but I can't read them. It's a rare condition called alexia with agraphia that only a few stroke victims have, so it hasn't been studied much. But rare as it is, it's irritating to not be able to read. That limitation alone has upended my life." Marsha frowned as she looked out the car window.

"I can't imagine how difficult that would be. Do the doctors think your reading ability might still come back?"

"They don't know," Marsha said as she shrugged her shoulders. "I'm in therapy twice a week with a speech and writing therapist, and she's hopeful. Between that and not being allowed to drive, I feel trapped inside my own body most of the time."

"So, you aren't allowed to drive because you can't read the road signs, right? That is a challenge." Dee glanced at her in the rearview mirror and smiled. "Well, I'm happy to be your driver today, Marsha! Before I picked you up, I was having a pretty spectacular pity party. I was complaining to God about being a single parent. I told him I didn't think it was fair that I'm the one struggling to make ends meet, while my ex is out there living any way he pleases. I'm so tired at the end of the day, I can hardly keep my eyes open long enough to fix dinner, give my son his bath, and look over his homework, not to mention my own. Yeah, I was driving along feeling really sorry for myself until you told me your story."

Marsha sat in silence for a moment, amazed at this fellow believer's honest revelation. She then said, "Dee, each of your so-called complaints is justified and real. As are mine. But, you're right. We both need to increase our thankfulness quotient, because we need to remember that things could always be much worse. I appreciate the reminder. I do. I know from experience that complaining about something, even something really hard, never makes me feel better.

And it never solves the problem. I'm going to make a pact with myself right now to stop complaining. In my heart and with my words. I'm going to pray for God to help me see the blessings in my trials. And I'll pray for you too!"

> The righteous person may have many troubles,
> but the Lord delivers him from them all.

If only our first response to any type of trial would be to close our eyes and silently give thanks to our always faithful, loving heavenly Father. If only. But, if we are honest, we'd have to admit that our first response to hardship isn't an expression of a thankful heart. Think how much sorrow we might spare ourselves if we gave thanks no matter how troubling the circumstance.

Let's be clear. I'm not saying we should be thankful we had a stroke or our spouse abandoned us, or whatever terrible thing has happened. What I'm saying is that God wants us to turn to him during these hopeless, frightening moments and thank him for being with us in the trial. God wants us to trust him with our desperate situations that from a human standpoint appear impossible to resolve. God desires for us as his beloved children to keep coming back to him for the strength, grace, and hope we need to carry on day by day.

Is it possible to be content in the midst of horrendous circumstances? Yes, it is. When we say yes, no matter how painful our situation, to God's will for our lives and we purpose to glorify him in the midst of life-altering situations, he then supernaturally buoys up our fragile hearts with faith, courage, and the power to see his goodness shine through even our darkest night.

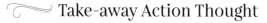

Take-away Action Thought

When you start to fall into a state of self-pity, stop your "stinking thinking"! Instead, intentionally begin giving thanks for every blessing of God that you can think of. Purposefully write down everything (small or large) for which you are grateful. Do not allow discontentment to fester in your heart.

My Heart's Cry to You, O Lord

Father, help me to never forget that difficult circumstances will try to reign over my heart and mind. Help me to discipline myself to think rightly about every hardship you allow to enter my life. I must counter my complaints with consistent thankfulness and contentment. Please give me the grace to obey you by giving thanks in all circumstances, because this is your will for me. Even though I may never understand why something is happening, please keep reminding me that you are with me in this battle. Help me to reframe any negative, hopeless thoughts with faith-fueled ones that honor you and show how much I trust in you and your plan for me. Amen.

Deliver Us

1. "I will extol the LORD at all times; his praise will always be on my lips. I will glory in the LORD; let the afflicted hear and rejoice." This week, purpose not to utter a single complaint. Instead, each time you are tempted to start complaining about your circumstances, counter those negative thoughts with words of gratitude.

2. "This poor man called, and the LORD heard him; he saved him out of all his troubles." Don't neglect to pray about anything that is troubling you, remembering that the Lord loves you and cares about every aspect of your life. Keep a running list of

prayer requests and their answers. Each day, set aside time to pray through your concerns and end by giving thanks to God, even before the answers come.

3. "The Lord is close to the brokenhearted and saves those who are crushed in spirit. The righteous person may have many troubles, but the Lord delivers him from them all." When you begin to throw yourself an unhelpful pity party, make an about-face and instead think about all the wonderful blessings with which God has surrounded you. Ask the Lord to help you transform your troubles into productive lessons in maturity and character growth.

The LORD is good to all;
    he has compassion on all he has made.
All your works praise you, LORD;
    your faithful people extol you. . . .

The LORD is trustworthy in all he promises
    and faithful in all he does.
The LORD upholds all who fall
    and lifts up all who are bowed down.
The eyes of all look to you,
    and you give them their food at the proper time.
You open your hand
    and satisfy the desires of every living thing.

The LORD is righteous in all his ways
    and faithful in all he does.
The LORD is near to all who call on him,
    to all who call on him in truth.

PSALM 145

CHAPTER 29

Being a Blessing to Others,
No Matter What

*Grant me to rest on thy power and faithfulness, and
to know that there are two things worth living for: to
further thy cause in the world, and to do good to the
souls and bodies of men. This is my ministry, my life, my
prayer, my end. Grant me grace that I shall not fail.*

PURITAN PRAYER

Vivian sat at her computer, gazing blankly at the upcoming week's calendar while her heart sank. It was only March and they'd had eight funerals already this year. She didn't know how many more days she could handle like these. They'd had two funerals that week alone. Vivian closed her eyes and stretched her neck as she exhaled deeply, feeling the tears burning her throat yet again.

Of course, she realized that it didn't matter how weary or sad she felt, there was a job to be done. As the senior pastor's wife, she was well acquainted with suffering as most of their church's members came directly to Carl and her whenever someone was in need. Vivian and Carl had been in ministry for over thirty years and had seen a lot. Now in their sixties, they were feeling their age and the weight of their fellowship's burdens more than ever before.

Well-meaning folks in the church had already told them they needed to step back a bit and allow other staff to pick up some of the responsibilities, and they had done so. But when it came to special occasions such as child dedications, baptisms, and marriages, their members wanted Pastor Carl to celebrate these life markers with them personally. The same principle applied when people were going through a crisis. Whether a fellow believer was facing a life-threatening illness, grieving the death of a loved one, or dealing with any number of life-altering scenarios, it was Pastor Carl they called on for advice, support, and prayer.

As Vivian looked back at the schedule, she knew that there were some roles and responsibilities they couldn't hand off to their staff, as wonderful as they were. And honestly, Vivian admitted to herself, she wouldn't want to. At that moment, she realized just how much she loved these dear people and how she wanted to help them carry the weight of their burdens. Resigned to continue on, she prayed for the Lord to keep her heart and mind focused on him alone that week, that she would remember that she relied solely on his strength as she helped others. It had always been that way and always would be.

> The LORD is righteous in all his ways
> and faithful in all he does.
> The LORD is near to all who call on him,
> to all who call on him in truth.

This story is a common tale among those who serve others in all kinds of capacities, not only those in full-time ministry positions. Every disciple of Jesus who seeks to live an other-oriented, servant-focused life will feel bone-tired at one time or another. You may even feel like this right now.

As we submit ourselves daily to the Lord's leading, we may feel that we're facing more tasks and responsibilities than we can reasonably accomplish. No matter what is on our must-do-today agenda, we know we have to rely on God's enabling strength, grace, wisdom, and supernatural empowerment to get the job done.

What serves us best is to acknowledge our moment-by-moment dependence on the Lord to accomplish whatever tasks he sets before us and be glad to be of use to his children as we live out his love. As Vivian so aptly prayed, may the Lord help us to keep our hearts and minds focused on him alone today and always. We must never believe for a minute that anything we do in service for others is done in our own strength. We need to pray this and then get to work because, as Vivian realized, there's a job to be done!

Read again the power-packed, life-altering, eternity-changing prayer at the beginning of this chapter that succinctly sums up what we desire most as we serve the Lord and seek to bring honor to his name. May we thank the Lord that we will not fail because he has promised to supply us with all we need to serve others well. Today. Tomorrow. Always.

Take-away Action Thought

When you begin to sink under the weight of all that has to be done, remove yourself from the busyness at hand and retreat to a quiet place to be alone with the Lord. Remind yourself that even Jesus, being God the Son, retreated to a solitary place when he was exhausted from ministering to the people.

My Heart's Cry to You, O Lord

Father, it's been another one of those weeks when I felt my heart begin to race whenever I received another call, text, or email. I feel completely undone by the traumatic events I have witnessed in these recent weeks. While I am grateful to help ease the burdens around me, I am emotionally exhausted. I've been crying for no reason, and I haven't been sleeping well. Please help me to be wise about what I say yes to as I try to serve others. But overall, help me to always turn to you for my strength, grace, and wisdom. I desire to serve others, but I know I need your supernatural enabling to succeed in this. Amen.

Deliver Us

1. "The LORD upholds all who fall and lifts up all who are bowed down." During this next week, set time aside to look ahead at the coming month. Then block off a specific time for personal rest and reflection, so that even though your ministry may be stressful during this season, you can be assured of these off-limit dates to regain your inner strength.

2. "The eyes of all look to you, and you give them their food at the proper time. You open your hand and satisfy the desires of every living thing." When you begin to feel weary and overwhelmed by the demands placed on you by others, take a step back to prayerfully consider your life, your calling, and specifically what you believe God is asking you to do. Remind yourself that God doesn't want you to burn yourself out. Rather, he promises to give you all that you need to sustain a healthy life.

3. "The LORD is near to all who call on him, to all who call on him in truth." Set aside a portion of each evening this week and commit yourself to Bible reading, prayer, and, most significantly, a time of quiet meditation. Copy down several verses that bring comfort to your heart and meditate on God's goodness to supply you with everything you need to serve him and others well.

Answer me when I call to you,
    my righteous God.
Give me relief from my distress;
    have mercy on me and hear my prayer. . . .

Know that the LORD has set apart his faithful servant for himself;
    the LORD hears when I call to him.

Tremble and do not sin;
    when you are on your beds,
        search your hearts and be silent.
Offer the sacrifices of the righteous
    and trust in the LORD.

Many, LORD, are asking, "Who will bring us prosperity?"
    Let the light of your face shine on us.
Fill my heart with joy
    when their grain and new wine abound.

In peace I will lie down and sleep,
    for you alone, LORD,
    make me dwell in safety.

PSALM 4

CHAPTER 30

Holding Jesus Dearer
Than Anything Else

Never allow yourself to complain about anything—not even the weather. Never picture yourself in any other circumstances or someplace else. Never compare your lot with another's. Never allow yourself to wish this or that had been otherwise. Never dwell on tomorrow—remember that is God's, not ours.

LINDA DILLOW

Last night I endured fits of sleeplessness and bad dreams, waking up feeling unrested and undone. As of yesterday, the coronavirus was still erupting in the early stages across our nation and throughout the world. No matter how much I try to keep up on new findings each day, it is the unknown that is the most terrifying aspect of this pandemic. I'm finding myself reading and then disbelieving what I'm reading, because it simply doesn't seem real. My world feels as though it has been upended, affecting my life (and yours) in every way possible.

While I am not afraid of contracting the virus and dying, I am being cautious. I am also being highly selective about what constitutes a "need" versus a "want" before venturing out. My parents are elderly and have some health issues, so my brother and I have firmly told them to stay put at home for the duration and that we will bring anything they need to them.

While I work from home and am grateful for this particular blessing, my husband is employed by the public-school system and my adult daughter is a social worker serving at a nearby public elementary school. This means that every time they ventured out to work they came into contact with hundreds of people. I have to say I was relieved when our state closed the schools until the authorities deemed it safe to reopen. But of course, at this moment, we don't know exactly how long that will be and this uncertainty seems to be the "new normal."

As I have been processing this ever-escalating global crisis, my heart has fluctuated between hope and despair, punctuated by moments of fear. There are so many what ifs in this constantly evolving scenario, it is exhausting to try and make sense of them all. Then this morning, weary from trying to figure out any of it, I gave up—and it was the best decision I've made all week. I realized that I don't have to have all the answers and I never will. All I truly need to calm my inner self is to settle down in the presence of the Lord and allow the richness of Scripture to provide the spiritual sustenance I need. So instead of compulsively reading every article out there on this virus or watching every news show, I am choosing instead to strengthen my inner person so I can handle whatever God allows in the coming days, weeks, months—and even years.

> In peace I will lie down and sleep,
>   for you alone, Lord,
>   make me dwell in safety.

While poring over Scripture today, I found that a common theme kept rising to the surface. First, God is in complete control. He is not sitting on a throne in heaven wringing his hands in surprise or despair. That truth alone shores up my heart and mind as I picture our faithful, all-powerful, ever-present heavenly Father presiding over all of heaven and earth. Second, because I am eternally secure in Jesus' perfect sacrifice for my sins on the cross, which means I am not afraid of dying, I can put my efforts into supporting, encouraging, and serving those around me.

After enduring a roller coaster of a week, I see now that I took my eyes off the Lord more than I care to admit—and, like Peter, began sinking beneath the stormy waves. It's as though I had been temporarily swept away by the uncertainty of this worldwide crisis. God help us to see the tremendous opportunities before us to be Jesus to others with our loving words and acts of service. Let's demonstrate that no matter how much we may have to give up during times of crisis, we know that people matter the most. Let's not grumble when we're asked to give up what we often take for granted. Let's be looking every single day for ways to lighten someone's load by helping them carry their burdens.

Let's know Jesus' peace for ourselves, and then let's make Jesus known to everyone around us. Let's show a desperate and broken world what really matters by holding Jesus dearer than anything else on earth. Amen.

Take-away Action Thought

When you are afraid, turn to the book of Psalms and allow God's perfect promises to quiet your heart and mind. Let the full range of the psalmists' emotions bring you comfort and encouragement. Then write down several passages you found that really spoke to you and lifted you up when you needed it most.

My Heart's Cry to You, O Lord

Father, I endured another restless night because I was anxious and afraid. I realize that I have no idea what tomorrow will bring, but you do. You are always in complete control and are ever present in our trials. Please help me to honor you, Lord, by trusting you during this time of worldwide fear and confusion. Lead me to that quiet stream where I can find refreshment and renewed strength. I need you, Lord. I need your comfort and strength, so I can forget about my own needs and look for ways to love and serve others. Father, I ask that you would enable me to lay down every single one of my worries and leave them with you. Let me rest through the night in your perfect provision and awaken ready to be Jesus' hands and feet tomorrow. Amen.

Deliver Us

1. "Answer me when I call to you, my righteous God. Give me relief from my distress; have mercy on me and hear my prayer." Morning and night this week, open your journal and write down whatever is troubling you. Be specific when you ask God to be merciful and give you the grace, strength, and peace to see these overwhelming events as completely under his perfect control.

2. "Know that the LORD has set apart his faithful servant for himself; the LORD hears when I call to him." Search for all the verses you can locate that speak of God hearing the prayers of his children. Write them down, speak them out loud, and begin memorizing them.

3. "In peace I will lie down and sleep, for you alone, LORD, make me dwell in safety." Each night before you go to sleep, ask for God's protection from head to toe. Ask him to protect your mind from terrifying dreams and to give you sweet rest all through the night, so you can awaken eager and ready to serve as God leads you.

ᖗ Sources for Quotations

1. Edward T. Welch, *Depression: A Stubborn Darkness* (Greensboro: New Growth Press, 2011), 97.

2. Ken Gire, *The North Face of God* (Colorado Springs: Tyndale, 2005).

3. Oswald Chambers, *My Utmost for His Highest* (Grand Rapids: Discovery House, 1992), February 21 entry.

4. Paul David Tripp, *New Morning Mercies: A Daily Gospel Devotional* (Wheaton, IL: Crossway, 2014), March 2 entry.

5. George MacDonald, *Annuals of a Quiet Neighborhood* (Glendale, CA: Bibliotech Press, 2019), 203.

6. Andrew Murray, in *1500 Illustrations for Biblical Preaching*, edited by Michael P. Green (Grand Rapids: Baker, 1982), 388.

7. Nancy Leigh DeMoss, *Choosing Gratitude: Your Journey to Joy* (Chicago: Moody, 2009), 23–24.

8. Arthur Bennett, ed., *The Valley of Vision: A Collection of Puritan Prayers and Devotions* (Carlisle, PA: Banner of Truth Trust, 2007), 270–71.

9. Jerry Bridges, *Trusting God* (Colorado Springs: NavPress, 1988), 127–28.

10. Tim Lane and Paul Tripp, *Relationships: A Mess Worth Making* (Greensboro: New Growth Press, 2006), 97.

11. DeMoss, *Choosing Gratitude*, 165.

12. Bridges, *Trusting God*, 28.

13. John MacArthur, *Anxious for Nothing* (Colorado Springs: David C. Cook, 2012), 33.

14. C. S. Lewis, in *Letters of C. S. Lewis*, edited by W. H. Lewis and Walter Hooper (Orlando: Harcourt Books, 1966), 477.

15. Randy Alcorn, *90 Days of God's Goodness: Daily Reflections That Shine Light on Personal Darkness* (Colorado Springs: Multnomah, 2011), 254.

16. DeMoss, *Choosing Gratitude*, 92–93.

17. Bridges, *Trusting God*, 140–41.

18. Elisabeth Elliot, *The Elisabeth Elliot Newsletter* (March/April 1995): 1.

19. Alcorn, *90 Days of God's Goodness*, 225.

20. Tripp, *New Morning Mercies*, January 14 entry.

21. Bridges, *Trusting God*, 197.

22. MacArthur, *Anxious for Nothing*, 32.

23. Nancy Leigh DeMoss, *Choosing Forgiveness: Your Journey to Freedom* (Chicago: Moody, 2008), 156.

24. Tripp, *New Morning Mercies*, January 12 entry.

25. Bridges, *Trusting God*, 178.

26. Bridges, *Trusting God*, 174.

27. Joni Eareckson Tada, *Hope . . . the Best of Things* (Wheaton, IL: Crossway, 2008), 195.

28. MacArthur, *Anxious for Nothing*, 129.

29. Bennett, *The Valley of Vision*, 343.

30. Linda Dillow, *Calm My Anxious Heart* (Colorado Springs: NavPress, 2007), 13.